It's All About You

It's All About You

Eeefy

ISBN: 978-1-7365522-0-9

Dedication

To The Almighty God—the sufficient grace that sustains me, and mercy that prevails over my life. You are ever responsible for everything I have achieved in life. I am a positive extension of Your image. All I ever want to be is a vessel of hope, a voice for the voiceless, and I pray that Your light continues to illuminate my path so that I shine, and men may see my good works and glorify You.

Chidi Ike, aka Chairman—My big brother, may your precious soul rest in the bosom of the Lord. My heart is wrenched at your passing, because you are a jewel and pride to the Ike family. You were very supportive in my journey here in Nigeria. I miss your encouraging words and advice. I miss you greatly! I love you.

Soroke Ike—My younger brother, who I also embrace as my spiritual son and heartbeat. Your love toward me is a propellant to my success here in Nigeria. You keep me focused and balanced in the spirit with your strength, compassion, wisdom, and continuous prayers. I believe and know that with you I will succeed! Thank you for the superior being that you are. I love you.

Chief Wilfred Akweke Ike (aka Ugochinyere 1 of Egbema Kingdom)—My father, your spirit echoes on my talents, my drive, my wisdom, my boldness, my dogged determination to prosper and be significant in society. Thank you for the friendship we share now. My future is brighter because of your love and encouragement. I love you.

Gladys Chinyere Ike—My precious mother and queen. A woman of indomitable spirit and great virtue, you have by your personality and discipline instilled in me the regal bearing of a queen and the sensitivity of a princess that have collectively helped to construct my character. Yes, you imbued in me the grace and style that I project with ease. I adore you so much, Mummy.

Chinelo Iwenofu—My spiritual mother, best friend, and guardian, you know a creative and ambitious soul like me can only succeed in structuring a healthy and successful lifestyle when I can dwell in a peaceful and loving environment which living with you has accorded me the opportunity to achieve. By your motherly love, friendship, demure personality, patience, and calm spirit, you have helped cultivate the balance and focus I possess in my spirit. By your intellect, creative prowess, and willingness to critique my writings, you have assured my messages of light are shared with the world. I am so grateful and eager to make you proud, Mummy. I love you to bits.

Foreword

Our modern world is inundated with very uninspiring events—wars, terrorism, crimes against humanity, kidnappings, robberies, murders, blackmails, and betrayals.

This uninspiring environment weighs negatively on the minds of people, particularly the youth, with its concomitant adverse effects of depression, hopelessness, crime, suicide, and other vices.

As Joseph Martino puts it, "The man and woman with sight see things as they are; the man and woman with insight see things as they could be."

This summarizes the mindset of great inspirational writers like Eeefy, who, despite their uninspiring environment, have risen to the lofty heights of inspiring others and motivating their minds toward seeing things as they could be. Yes, she believes that the earth could be a beautiful Garden of Eden where love dominates the hearts of men and everybody gets the opportunity to realize their cherished dreams in freedom, civility, and decorum.

By her inspirational words and works, hope is brought to the hopeless, direction to the confused, contentment to the greedy, high esteem to men of low esteem, and joy to the depressed.

I, therefore, recommend this book to all who want to attain their purpose in life in a cultured, enlightened, and inspired way.

Kenneth Okonkwo
Legal Practitioner/Movie Actor

CONTENTS

Synopsis · · · 1
It's All About You · · · 2
Celebrating The Glory in You · · · 3
Intention and Motivation · · · 5
Devil's Games · · · 6
Consistency is Essential to Success · · · 7
Genuine Connection · · · 8
Oneness · · · 9
Tone of Voice · · · 10
Being Suppressed · · · 11
Purpose-Driven Activities · · · 12
Narcissism · · · 15
My Existence · · · 17
The Reason for Your Struggles · · · 18
Why are We Stimulated by Danger and Mediocrity? · · · 19
Class in Status · · · 20
Womanhood · · · 21
Warm Reception · · · 23
What Little Things Mean to The Oppressed · · · 24
Forgiving The Past · · · 25
Your Significance in Life · · · 26
Skin Color · · · 27
He/She Will Never Succeed · · · 29
You are a Captive of Your Declared Enemy · · · 30
Interpretation · · · 31
Independence Day of America—4Th of July · · · 32
Freedom · · · 33
Relating With People · · · 34
Retiring Young · · · 35

Sex Trafficking· 36
The Power of Your Essence· 38
Misunderstanding and Misapplication of Culture · · · · · · · · · · · · · · 39
Bride Price · 40
Hating on a Giver · 42
Hiding Behind Fake Profiles · 43
Parents' Perception of Their Children · 45
The Subjugation of Women · 46
There's Real Security in Self-Reliance! · 48
Do You Sacrifice Your Happiness and Comfort to Help Others? · · · · 49
Greed in High Places ·51
Men, You Can Provoke The Nagging· 54
More Causes of Nagging · 55
Your Identity · 56
People Around Government Officials Who Extort Money
From Others to Make Introductions · 57
The World is My Oyster · 59
September 11—Great America· 60
Poverty of The Spirit ·61
Celebrating Your Parents · 62
Wardrobes and Image · 63
Choice · 64
Act of Thinking · 65
Alternative · 66
A Toxic Environment is Extensively Destructive · · · · · · · · · · · · · · 67
Make-Believe · 68
Blind Comparison · 69
Defensive Approach · 70
What Happens When You Wake Up One Day And You Are
No Longer In Charge? · 71
Purge Your Environment · 72
Govern What Transpires in Your World· ·74
The Weak Associates · 75

The Power of Gratitude 76
Cyber Preying Mantis 77
Your Attitude 78
The Employer 79
Quality Company 80
Manipulating The Mind 82
Doubting Your Mate 83
Your Sick Spouse 84
Angry Over Trivialities 85
Life Can Be Unfair 86
Fulfilling Leadership Qualities 87
Oil is Not Everything 89
What to Do in A Chaotic Polygamous Family 91
Marrying Multiple Wives 92
Death 93
Do You Need to Be Drawing a Line? 94
Personal Transformation 95
Giving The Audience Something Not to Be Bored About 96
Beware of Small-Minded Jealousy 97
Getting Frustrated Often? 98
Know Yourself 99
Ambition 100
Solitude 101
Enjoying One's Own Company 102
Be in Tune With The Spirit 103
Gift of The Gab 104
Instincts 105
Potential Dangers in Surrogacy 106
Absentmindedness 108
Unrealistic Expectations From New Mate 109
Forget Seeking A Perfect Mate! 110
Letting Go 111
Yelling When Angry is a Natural Human Inclination 112

Explore Your God-Given Talents 113
Disturbed Spirits 114
Wish 116
Structure and Balance 117
New Goal 118
Peripherals—A Distraction 119
Evil Act Has No Limit 120
"Over My Dead Body!" 121
Do You Want Your Presence Or Absence to Be Celebrated? 122
Falling in Love With Your Tormentor 123
Noisy Environment and its Negative Effects 124
Irrelevant Advice 126
Chain of Kindness 127
Chain of Evil 128
Do Not Let The Evil Ones Change Your Good Heart 129
The Contents of Your Soul 130
Are Your Energy and Skills for Destruction? 131
Associating With Failure Can Lead to Failure 132
Incident of Insensitivity 133
No Common Sense? 134
Do You Underestimate Your Potential? 135
Spirit of Leadership 136
Looking Down on Someone 137
Communication Between Couples 138
Challenges Reveal Weaknesses 140
The Splendor of The Concept 141
Unconscious Limitations 142
Weave Wearing and Fake Hair Loving is Not Particular to Black Women 143
Help 144
Naivety 145
The Fire Brigade Approach 146
Do You Have The Ability to Survive and Thrive? 147

Communication in a Relationship · 148
The Downfall of a Man is not The End of His Life · · · · · · · · · · · · · ·149
Mediation ·150
Do You Wish to Become Someone Else? ·151
Your Infinite Potential ·152
Life Force ·153
The Destructive Element of Words ·154
Physically Nourishing The Spirit ·155
To Fight is Sometimes to Die ·156
Your Woman's or Man's Evil Friends ·157
The Effect of Listening in a Relationship ·158
Reevaluation ·159
Courage · 160
To Heal Someone Emotionally ·161
What Kind of Future Would you Have With a Violent Mate? · · · · · ·162
Your Mate Straying Away From You · 164
We are all Different · 166
Charity Begins at Home ·167
What is The Real Cause of Your Problem? · · · · · · · · · · · · · · · · · · · 168
Depths of Your Soul ·169
Your Eagerness to Succeed ·170
Hold Firm to Your Great Ideas ·171
Jobless Critics ·172
Pregnant for a Man Other Than Your Husband? · · · · · · · · · · · · · · ·174
Life is Forward ·175
Parents, Try to Listen to Your Children ·176
Only a Foolish Boy Abandons His Pregnant Mate · · · · · · · · · · · · · 177
Your Purpose ·178
Living From Your Essence ·179
The Wicked Sister-In-Law · 180
The Dawning of a New You ·181
Well-Being ·182
Comfort in Extreme Poverty ·185

Can We Try to Get Along? or Do You Relish Conflicts? 186
Anger Over Nonsensical 187
Character Flaw 188
Limitation 189
Natural Hair 190
Peace Within 192
Change 193
The Grace of Perfection in Man 194
Rebuilding Your Confidence 195
The Consciousness of Love 196
Your Girlfriends 197
Passion 198
Growth 199
My Journey 200
Fans Comments 202
Beautiful One 205

Synopsis

The ever porous mind of Eeefy, the most charming and charismatic author of the *IT'S ALL ABOUT YOU*, who wakes up every day filled with inspirational prose and eager to share her thoughts on *social media*. with positive inspirational anecdotes that detract from the popular gossip and criticism meted out by users. She motivates her fans and the readers on how to deal with the intricacies of life and receives a barrage of grateful replies in return.

A *social media* heroine, who has attracted numerous fans. She is indeed the queen of networking, with her magnificent photographs that keenly draw her admirers from all over the world.

IT'S ALL ABOUT YOU is indeed a deep reflection of her interpretation of the conflicts in one's existence. An intriguing piece of creative masterpiece that is in tune with modern day living and reaches out to the spiritual consciences of a flexible and discerning reader.

Introducing a new trend and style in reading drama, from a glamorous motivational speaker and life-coach poised to draw attention for all the right reasons. Words of wisdom to be referred to and read, bringing real life solutions closer than ever, not just electronically but now also in print.

It's All About You

Every day, I wake up with one thought.
My mind has one direction:
The need to heal.
The need to inspire.
The need to shed light where there is darkness.
The need to lift up broken spirits,
The need to impart joy.

So I start thinking.

I ponder deeply about any situation that springs forth in my analytical mind concerning humankind.

It could be an issue I addressed with an old client, an observation from conversations with people, personal experiences, fans, friends, films, TV shows, documentaries, etc.

It is always about analyzing life.
Making a difference.
Effecting a change!
It is always about you!

Celebrating The Glory in You

Celebrating the glory within you simply means celebrating the beauty in you. Everyone possesses great qualities that are unique to them. Yes, God made each of us different from the other. The problem is that we are too focused on celebrating or envying the glory of another instead of looking inward to discover our own beauty and celebrate it. When you start to celebrate your own beauty, it will reflect in your dispositions. Your outward projection is a reflection of your inner feelings. When you recognize and appreciate the uniqueness in you, then the world around you would recognize and appreciate it too.

Your glory is different from the glory of your neighbor. No two people have the same glory.

The reason you recognize a person's glory is because the person first recognized and expressed it through their disposition, or someone else perceived a clue of it and helped the person discover and project it to the world, just like the great men and women we admire, or the celebrities we celebrate. Now, it does not mean that they do not have challenges. We all do, as challenges are the catalyst to growth.

There are valid reasons that keep people from discerning their glory, and we must address those reasons so that we can all find a path to healing and living a fulfilled life.

First, it starts with your foundation as an individual. If you are reared in an environment of abuse, it will inevitably suppress your spirit and thereby make it difficult or impossible to realize your special qualities.

Abuse is a monster with different faces, including neglect, rejection, mental and emotional abuse, physical abuse, and so on. It can eventually be exacerbated by failure, disappointments, and many more challenges.

But I tell you that all of these phenomena that are deterrents could also aide your growth, if well managed. We must not dwell on our weak childhoods, past failures, or bad experiences. We must not keep believing that we are nothing, because we are not like the rich or the famous or the popular students in school. We must rise from that dark pit to where there is light and abundance, because there is abundance for the children of God.

"Arise, shine, for your light has come,
and the glory of the Lord rises upon you."

—Isa. 60:1

Yes, my brothers and sisters, the glory is in, you and you must look inward to realize it! You must see your failures and bad experiences as catalysts to your growth. You must take authority over your struggles. You must believe you are unique and there is no one like you! You must believe you are specially and wonderfully made so that you can flourish! The world is waiting to experience your light so celebrate your glory!

Intention and Motivation

What is your intention for your future? Do you have the desire for success? If you are ambitious, the first thing you ought to do is discover your skills and understand your potential for success. Observing your skills should by itself be a motivation to pursue success, because then you know that you possess the capacity needed to attain a great height.

Every skill has to be developed to the highest level of appreciation, and awareness of your talents is thus the first step. The next step is to cultivate that skill, which will require discipline, focus, perseverance, and consistency, as you will expectedly confront trials and errors that could be discouraging but helpful in building your character and procuring valuable perspective to your goal.

Motivation is an elusive phenomenon where one lacks skills. Intention and motivation can be cultivated through ambition. Many people lack the desire to succeed because of the work required to achieve such aim. Those who lack the spirit of ambition almost always remain stagnant in the spirit and resolve to begging and living on handouts.

I wonder if the unambitious ever take the time to think about what it will be like to uphold the position of success and the noble role of aiding others in need. I wonder if they possess the level of pride that should be motivation for ambition! I believe that pride should actually stimulate the desire for success. I find it ridiculous when someone who lacks the skills and the desire to work exhibits the spirit of pride. Pride for what, exactly?

Devil's Games

When your intentions are great and especially extensive, the devil will exploit your weaknesses, challenge your strengths, and use your friends, associates, co-workers, business partners—your trusted people within your very own domain—even your family members and your partner. Anyone can be employed as a vessel to stop your mission, so you must be persistently focused on your vision and work to achieve your great goals.

The Devil does not like goodness in all its forms!

Consistency is Essential to Success

Consistency is a compelling force to success.

Consistency reveals seriousness.

Consistency is a reflection of discipline.

Consistency reveals the height of one's passion for the intended goal.

Consistency attracts and inspires support.

Consistency is admirable.

Consistency is a cumulation of desire, belief, and focus, in spite of challenges.

Consistency is the strength that binds, introducing absolute cohesion.

We must adopt the habit of consistency to succeed in any intended goal in life, and even when one is simply being oneself but possesses a unique mannerism or projects an image that may be peculiar in society, one would be appreciated eventually if the exhibited character is consistent.

Stay consistent, for you will eventually achieve success and be appreciated in your own right!

Genuine Connection

Are you able to connect with someone sincerely and free of preconceptions from old experiences, whether good or bad? Yes, even positive experiences can misguide and lure one into a new and crooked journey! A warped judgment of character is not always engendered by negative experiences. It is also caused by lack of challenges that develop wisdom and inspire growth; thus, one is also inclined to prejudice.

It is essential for you to have a genuine connection with someone and by so doing allow yourself to operate from your core where compassion lies. When you treat someone with sincerity, it should naturally inspire a certain level of genuineness in the person that will consequently produce a healthy relationship between the two of you that will also affect the lives of those around you, as our treatment toward a person is naturally extensive.

Many of us hamper our happiness and that of others by our insincerity in friendship and by prejudice. We connect with a person from a polluted part of our soul and subsequently contaminate the fellow's spirit or provoke a personality disorder that will only translate into many other problems.

Oneness

If we are all created by one God, it means we are all rooted in one spirit! Why then do we cultivate and nurture so much hatred and disdain for fellow human beings? Why do we eagerly condemn people for their skin color? Why religious war? Does our God not see that we kill each other in the process of making our supplications to Him or pretending to revere Him?

I believe that synergy is the ultimate method to accomplish goals, fulfill destinies, and live a meaningful life, as we all need other people's potent spirit to conceive ideas, produce and develop the concept of our vision, encourage our goals, and lend us different and inspiring perspectives of life and our ambitions.

There can never be war in oneness! Yes, I would never want to trouble someone in accord with me. The peace I feel from a person should only inspire me to treat the fellow with love and respect, and if I feel to do otherwise, then I need help, as that evil I feel only reflects a wicked or evil soul.

Tone of Voice

One's manner of speaking can be hereditary. This can result in unintended consequences; sometimes, the intention is not to be harsh in tone, but the inborn manner of speaking takes dominion and maybe an abrasiveness of tone changes the context of the message being conveyed.

Yes, those who have had the opportunity to know you over a period of time can adapt to your usual range of tones, but new acquaintances, new associates, and even new friends will very probably misunderstand you.

So be aware of these possible problems, as it is a factor in communication, which is obviously an innate element in personal interaction and socialization.

Being Suppressed

It is frustrating if you possess skills and great attributes and are willing to impart them on other people but individuals try to create impediments for you. Of course, it is usually the inferior leaders and inferior people in power who are guilty of such wicked behavior, as they are eager to manipulate, exploit, abuse and cause sorrow. They are discouraging even though what you have to offer is useful. They want to siphon your blood by placing draconian conditions on you, because they lack appreciation for life and happiness. They are afraid of your success and the possibility that you may not need them anymore, and then they would no longer have someone around to massage their ego or someone to look down upon.

Inferior leaders and inferior people in power mostly prefer their subordinates or people in their vicinity to stay destitute so that they could have full control and have someone beneath them that they can oppress. It also, in a sick kind of way, elevates their confidence. Is that really confidence, or does it solidify the mask they are wearing to shield their weaknesses? Darling, I still believe that even if you wear the most concrete and expensive mask, your weaknesses will be glaring to an alert soul!

It is important that those of you who are victims of these inferior people in power do not recede from your need to accomplish your meaningful goals. You may have to reevaluate your strategy and perhaps change environment, if it is necessary or critical for you to do so. But do not, I repeat, do not withdraw or wallow in failure and disappointment, as they are also deterrents to your success and happiness. Determination, consistency, and faith will eventually attract the genuine people to you.

Purpose-Driven Activities

Do you spend time on things that are relevant to your purpose?

Do you know your purpose?

Do you know what God says regarding you?

Every day is to be spent pursuing your purpose, including days of meditation and prayer to God, because you must thank God for your life and His will for you and ask Him for clarity and guidance to travel your journey; in fact, that is an integral component of pursuing your purpose.

You must not be afraid to embark on your journey to realize your purpose, even if you feel incompetent for any reason. Your inability to do things that are necessary should provoke the need to learn, and it is the actual point of one's life that necessitates growth, so you must learn to force yourself into confronting those challenges. In doing so, you will eventually gain the skills required to travel your journey.

The problem is not the lack of skill but the presence of fear and low self-esteem. This type of fear is usually a fear of failure; most people live a life of stagnation, because they are afraid to fail. Failure can be a valuable component of growth, as many great people have failed before they became successful. One must know that failure can be part of the process of growth, else the spirit remains unchallenged and even stagnant.

Fear is bondage and an impediment to growth, so if you are afraid to take steps toward your journey, you should first work hard to eradicate the spirit of fear. For example, think of yourself as a little toddler who is just learning to walk, the excited way in which they attempt to walk taking a few steps at a time, stumbling and falling, getting up and continuing to fall down, and taking more steps till they become stronger and longer, until they become firm, permanent steps. That is life! Not succumbing to failure. Now, the way to banish it is to accept the fact that failure is not the problem but part of the journey of life.

The fear of failure stems from low self-esteem. The feeling of incompetence reflects a low estimation of yourself. So you lack the skills required to do something. Does that mean you are less of a person? It just means you are either pursuing a career not meant for you, or it is truly your purpose but you have to acquire the required skills. Therefore, you need to learn, period! When people have a burning desire, they find a way. "Necessity is the mother of invention," as they say.

I, for instance, understand that my purpose is to deliver messages of light through my own clarifications, and to do so, I must be able to ponder deeply on issues to gain true understanding. The ability to peer through the depths of situations can only be possible with focus, and focus is gained through tranquility. Therefore, I need to dwell in a peaceful environment and have a great level of control over what transpires in my world. After gaining clarity, I need to be able to convey my understanding in a comprehensible language, thus the need to learn the use of English, which is the universal language. With all this in mind, I try every minute of every day to practice these collective factors, and that also means I focus on activities that are pertinent to my journey.

Spending your time on activities that are irrelevant to your journey can only detract from your purpose, even if you understand your purpose. Thus, it is critical to be focused. Do you know that focus tends to reveal important information and most likely other methods needed to accomplish a task? Yes, the act of focusing is a compelling view into the depth of a subject, thus revealing every dimension that applies to that subject. It is amazing what can be accomplished and how far one can go in achieving one's purpose when there is focus. Real focus is the result of passion, and a full life that is driven by passion is achievable when there is an objective that really is your true purpose such that you become driven by a burning desire to succeed!

Narcissism

Pride and vanity are often used interchangeably, but pride is what one thinks about self, while vanity is what one wishes people to think.

Unfortunately, society compels vanity into people's spirit through its unrealistic expectations, and then the media's relentless advertisement of that factor as the guiding principle of lifestyle also demands the fervent pursuit of the vanity. Now, this harsh reality in the society also tends to influence people's perception of pride. Pride is healthy, as it is simply the appreciation of self and is necessary to appease the spirit and aid in building one's self-esteem, which is a propellant to life and success.

Now, there is pride that reflects one's appreciation of self and accomplishment, while there is pride that reveals arrogance or conceit. People tend to misconstrue these two types of pride, especially when you threaten their insecurity or reveal their weakness through your strength. People of character and strength should appreciate another person's pride in their accomplishment and not be repulsed by it.

It is almost impulsive to take pride in your accomplishments, especially when you ascended from chronic struggles and pain, an experience that could extinguish the life of so many. Yes, I can relate to that fact, because I am so proud of myself for having the ability and willingness to yield to the calling of the Holy Spirit to strip off the garment of the victim and adorn the garment of a victor. Even that journey to healing was intense, as I sometimes regressed out of fear of what the future holds; fear of what my family or people around me may say; fear of what malicious critics may likely accuse me of. But then again, I realized that the future may be brighter than I thought and that all of those I feared for their viewpoints also have their own demons to deal with and are not better than me and cannot dictate my destiny.

I will succinctly say that arrogance is a mask that shrouds weakness. Arrogance reflects a superiority complex, and a superiority complex stems from an inferiority complex, and that is a weakness of spirit.

My Existence

I am grateful for my existence. I relish the life I am lucky to have. Every moment is a gift. Every success is a gift. Every failure is essential for my growth.

My agonies are brief, because I flourish under the shadow of my faith in God. My destiny has already been ordained in heaven, thus no power on earth can stop me.

I am blessed with a wonderful family and amazing friends. I am blessed with you. I love you.

The Reason for Your Struggles

It can be rather encouraging and empowering when you know why you are struggling and what you are struggling for. Yes, it is easier to deal with your challenges when you know that the reasons for those struggles are on your path to attain your destiny. That awareness tends to give you the hope and vision to keep on fighting, because one day—perhaps even in the very near future—that goal will be accomplished.

It is harder when you are struggling without a cause, when you are living in virtual oblivion, lacking understanding of why you exist and why you are struggling. Many people wake up every day without having a real goal in life and then retire to bed without actually accomplishing anything and with nothing to look forward to the next day. They have no task to challenge and stimulate their minds, no completed work or successful project to celebrate that would bring fulfillment to the spirit and inspire their confidence to reach a significant goal. Such stagnant spirits are prone to depression and are definitely vulnerable to exploitation, leading to many of the problems in our society.

You should have a dream, a goal to accomplish, and challenging activities that aid your mental growth . . . You should know why you are struggling and what for.

Wake up every day with your ultimate goal in mind, plan the day's tasks to accomplish, and really work for your purpose. Let your struggles and efforts be for your destiny!

Why are We Stimulated by Danger and Mediocrity?

It is unfortunate that we tend to be most stimulated by danger, mediocrity, and things that are devoid of inspiration and goodness. Even fictional films that are created for entertainment can inspire evil because of their strong mental effect. We tend to gravitate toward the evil nuances of the story rather than the undertone of its enlightenment or the palpable inspirational messages. We can also derive positive inspiration from horrific stories, though it is very risky; it depends on our level of understanding, state of mind, and the potency or weakness of our soul.

Evil has an impact if your soul is not potent enough to sift through the negative messages or if you are not able to detect the positive messages due to your contrived reasoning or past experiences. Thus, it is healthier to watch films that literally convey positive messages so that we only expose our minds to healthy images and stories.

The youths are more vulnerable to such negative effects, because their minds are not developed enough to understand the danger. Instead, they absorb everything seemingly exciting and may even practice them later, believing them to be cool and somehow acceptable.

Class in Status

I think class due to status is formulated by those in control who want to maintain control.

Ranking people in levels and class is part of how society is structured. It is done according to socioeconomic groups, making people easier to monitor. There are usually three levels of class: lower class, middle class, and upper class.

In some societies, class is also ranked by race. For example, in South Africa during the apartheid regime, the black Africans are ranked as the lowest, the middle class are the mixed races, Indians, and Chinese, while the upper or ruling class were the Caucasian whites. This maintained the status quo that the Anglo-Saxon or Aryan race—usually composed of European English or German descent—were looked at as the supreme race. Ridiculous!

In God's eyes everyone is born equal and on the same level, although we can all be distinguished by our very skin color, race, and most especially purpose. God identifies us by our purpose, which is His will for our existence as individuals.

Womanhood

Woman is the highest form of evolution. She replenishes the world, because she is the womb. She is the state of being. Without her, there would be none. She is the universe. Her place is to be in tune with nature. She does not need to fight but does need to be aware of who she is so that she can be tranquil and walk in divine light and beauty. She has to do what it takes to heal herself when necessary and through that nurture others.

As a woman, you hold the position of authority. You govern the people and thereby the places and things of the people. It is your responsibility to carry out the duties of life and to heal the world. You are Mother Nature. The world's subsistence is simply because of the height of your spirit and the potency of your strength. You have the aptitude to nurture a man to greatness, which should be your goal. Though you also possess the power to reduce him to the lowest factor of life, you should never manipulate your power in such a way, as that would only lead to destruction.

For you to be able to carry out your duties in life, you must dwell in a healthy environment, for you cannot flourish in a toxic one. You must endeavor to emancipate yourself from abusive relationships.

I love the power of a real man, as he has the spirit to protect and provide security for his family and those around him. One of the reasons for male dominance and inequality between men and women is because women have not taken their rightful place in life. The reason is that women have actually not really been taught their role in life. Hence, the man cannot grasp the woman's true stance, and when the woman falls short of her responsibilities, the man becomes confused.

A man can only have a perfect union and cocreate with a woman when he is balanced in his spirit. That means you as a man have to be familiar with both your masculine and feminine side. As a woman, your communication with your man can stimulate his feminine side, which is the sensitivity he needs to balance his spirit. Your love, patience, tolerance, and understanding will subdue his ego and inspire his compassion.

Egoism, abuse, manipulation, and superiority complexes reflect weakness of spirit and not the strength men believe they need to project.

When there is balance between couples, they would be able to raise healthy children. It is impossible to create responsible children in a toxic environment. Man needs to work in harmony with woman in all aspects of life so that both can reach their full potential for the good of all.

"For had they been of us, no doubt they
would have continued with us."

—1 Jn 2:19

Warm Reception

It is only healthy to treat people in the business world with warmth and respect. Unfortunately, that kind gesture could be exploited to your detriment, especially in a society that lacks structure and balance, a society where there are no protocols or disciplinary measures entrenched in companies because of lack of advancement, a society where a lot of people are poor in spirit and care less about their fellow human beings, with selfish attitudes ruling their interactions with customers, not customer service.

Future plans and long-term business relationships are not factors for consideration when stupidity is in control. May God grant us the grace to interact with others in a healthy manner!

What Little Things Mean to The Oppressed

It is quite astounding the energy and power unleashed from people who have been oppressed for a long time. When they are given a very little freedom or gain acceptance or achieve a little success, or their surroundings and lifestyle are slightly enhanced, it is quite a big deal to them, and it makes a big difference to their lives.

Yes, it is difficult to understand that the significance of your life can only be realized in your freedom and improved purpose when you are living or have lived in mental, spiritual, emotional, or physical bondage, and your environment is very unhealthy.

Little things are naturally amplified by conditions, such as mental, emotional, financial, or even physical conditions, even when one is going through healing or progressing. Therefore, immense relief and gratitude is felt when a gesture is made to eliminate some of the discomfort. Better infrastructure and heightened sense of self-worth does wonders for the psyche and raises self-esteem tremendously, especially when there is a leader that is sharp and knows how to make his people happy.

Have you ever given food to someone who is impoverished and then immediately experienced the energy rush from that person? It is a thrill and is quite inspiring, especially when you are one who lacks appreciation or takes for granted the good life you have and the opportunity you have been granted to have three square meals a day.

After being without for so long, some people learn to appreciate the small things in life and not to take anything for granted, even if they are given amenities for which they have really always been entitled to but are simply grateful when they experience an improvement in their way of life.

Forgiving The Past

We are supposed to forgive ourselves for our past wrongdoings and also hope that our new mate forgives us as well. But what if your past is despicable and grave? Would you be willing to share it with your mate, or would you rather keep it secret?

Yes, the past has a way of hounding the future, but in some cases, it is rather prudent to only share the past when it is absolutely necessary to do so. You may provoke a very bad reaction from your mate if you share your awful past at the wrong time, so leave it alone unless it is absolutely necessary.

The wrong time may be when your mate is undergoing emotional crisis or personal challenges or even expecting your perfect character to continue due to your behavior and their grasp of your personality. These aforementioned factors may not even be known to you, which can individually influence their judgment of anything, and that includes the story of your awful past. Hence, you need to demonstrate caution and careful consideration.

The right or very necessary moment to tell your mate about your past is usually at the inception of the relationship. How you approach it is also very critical, because the goal is to gain your mate's understanding and prevent any future crises that may result from the same unfortunate past.

Your Significance in Life

Your significance in life is not in your similarity to another but in your point of difference from another.

For you to be outstanding in life, you must stand out! This is the reason God put that gift in you to stand you out. For in everyone lies the seed of greatness. For the difference between ordinary and extraordinary is the extra.

Go the extra mile, and you will be outstanding. Stop thinking your gifts cannot be used because of the climate of hostility around you. Such climate will magnify the reward of that gift in you.

May God grant you understanding.

Skin Color

It is unfortunate that beauty is often judged by the skin color instead of by the soul of a person, which may not be instantly discernible but is more potent. Now, is it not paradoxical that many people detest dark skin, yet race to tanning salons during the winter and to the beach in the summer to darken their skin? Why are we so hypocritical to the point that we decry what we know deep down in our hearts we seek? Every skin color is beautiful and so should be appreciated. Those that abhor dark skin are those with limited knowledge, self-hate, prejudice, and confusion.

It is a shame that even a mother will condemn or belittle her own child, an expression of her own image because of her skin color! To all you ignorant mothers, the problem is not with your children and the color of their skin; the problem is with you, your weakness, and your distorted thinking for allowing yourself to be influenced by the ignorance and wickedness of the world around you.

Should your life and that of your dark-skinned children be dictated by others? Do you realize that your weakness is hampering your happiness and growth and that of your children? Are you aware of what really transpires in the world you live in? Do you understand that the devil has taken possession of many weak souls in this world, and those souls are vessels being exploited for evil? You sons and daughters of evil, you are the vile ones, not those you condemn for the color of their skin.

I am gorgeous in my own way, just as you are gorgeous in yours, and every skin color is gorgeous and the container of our beautiful souls. Look past your skin color, because where true beauty lies is in your core being. If we have to be restricted to judging others, then look at one's own actions. Those are the manifestation of one's soul, not their skin color. I would not elaborate further on this matter, because such prejudiced and possessed spirits mostly need deliverance and not just enlightenment. This judgment based on skin color is indeed spiritual madness.

He/She Will Never Succeed

REALLY? Do you think you are powerful enough to rewrite the destinies of those you wish evil? In fact, the moment you begin to nurture evil thoughts against your victim, God withdraws the authority and dominion He bestowed upon you as His child. Your evil thoughts cast a shadow in your heart, create a void in your spirit, and derail your own destiny.

Do not be deceived by your little ego, for light overwhelms darkness.

You are just a weak spirit the devil is exploiting for evil, and when he is done with the destruction of your pathetic soul, he will discard you and pick up another agent of darkness. May I inform you that Satan is constantly on the hunt for weak souls like yours to carry out his mischief, and he has no power to enthrone you to glory but to dethrone you into the pits of hell.

You can never achieve your full potential when you are busy peddling malicious gossip against your victims and plotting and wishing them evil.

The failure you wish your victim can never elevate your life or grant you power and glory; rather, it will condemn your life. BE warned!

You are a Captive of Your Declared Enemy

What occupies your heart and mind controls you, as it consciously and unconsciously influences your activities; even more so when the subject infuriates your spirit.

Therefore, when you detest someone or something too much and are constantly thinking of them, wishing them evil, or planning evil toward them, it means you are under their indirect governance, and this control is destructive to your life. It will deform your spirit and plunge it into the darkness that will only cast shadows on your path. Yes, you then become a captive of your enemy. You are a victim to your victim!

Interpretation

Your interpretation of a topic could differ from another person's interpretation and even from the intent of the conveyor of that message, because your understanding as an individual is likely to be influenced by your state of mind. Yes, the condition of the mind tends to influence one's perception of things and people, hence the varied discernment from person-to-person.

Sometimes, a clear message can also seem ambiguous to a person whose mind is plunged into crisis or someone who is distracted in the spirit and so cannot perceive the essence of the message, in spite of its nature.

I have also noticed the natural inclination of the mind to focus on a particular aspect of the message and make an assessment from that without considering the other factors that integrates the message with the intended meaning.

Even your feelings of hate or jealousy toward the communicator can also influence your understanding and judgment of the message, so be careful not to dismiss a good message that may illuminate your life and the life of your loved ones.

Independence Day of America—4th of July

Happy Independence Day to my family and friends in America . . . Beautiful country, God's own nation.

I am grateful for the quality and substance America instilled in me by the culture and structure of living. I am grateful for all the friends and people I met in America that impacted my life in one way or the other.

To my understanding, the American way of life will either compel your growth or plunge you into oblivion, depending on your state of mind and desires of life. Some want to grow and be significant to the society, while some would rather remain stagnant and most likely become a nuisance to society. Those who want to be significant and relevant contribute to society, even at the smallest levels.

We must understand that our existence is not meant to destroy but to be creative and productive and fruitful, so let us appreciate the opportunities we have to be alive while relishing our time on earth.

I appreciate the great men and women that led the American independence, for life has no meaning without liberty.

Freedom

Freedom is synonymous with goodness. Yes, your heart is at liberty when your every action is inclined to positivity and good. Your soul is peaceful and free of guilt of hurting others. This type of freedom is an elusive phenomenon in this intricate world—a world pervaded with challenges, trials, and tribulations that tend to pollute the heart and deplete it of its good qualities. So many people may feel the need and even make efforts to possess this type of freedom, but due to the harsh realities of life, the wicked souls they cross paths with deprive them of such virtue.

However, it is important for us to be cognizant of the extensive ramifications of these evil actions, reactions, and impulsions.

Relating With People

Do not look down on people. Do not see people the way they are but the way they could be. If you do, then you will relate with them in a healthier manner.

Do not look down on someone regarded as being from a lower class simply because the person is poor or has not acquired your level of education. People's backgrounds differ. Some will work themselves into greatness, and some will achieve greatness through luck. There are those who acquired it and yet fell, because they could not sustain greatness.

We should all share what we can do to uplift others. Even a simple piece of advice can guide another person to success.

Retiring Young

There are people that believe you should retire as soon as you have acquired enough financial wealth and then just enjoy life. Well, I do not believe in this unless you are at the reasonable age of retirement. Why should you rest on your laurels when you are still able and young? What if you are confronted with a grave challenge that demands most of the money you have saved? What would you do then?

It is normal to slow down after great achievements, because perhaps you are the type that had to work tirelessly for many years. Yes, you deserve rest and nurturing but not complete retirement when you are still young, unless, of course, you retire from one assiduous career to a more fun, laid-back career. In fact, a purpose-driven career should be more appropriate and fulfilling at such a stage of your life.

It is important to keep working, because challenging the mind to complete a task allows the spirit to flourish. Keeping the mind intellectually active actually prolongs your lifespan. The mind stalls when it is not being used. Even if it is a hobby you indulge in, it is vital to continuously challenge your mind.

It is okay to retire from hard work when one has reached what I call the "fifth stage" of human growth, which is reverting to the childhood stage when you are declining to the genesis of one's nature. It is not advisable to just completely retire at young age period!

Are you curious about the stages of growth? The five stages are: Childhood, Teenagehood, Adulthood, Maturity stage and Childhood Again.

Sex Trafficking

Sex trafficking is an industry that has proven impossible to eradicate due to the wealth the perpetrators and even some of the prostitutes amass as a result. Perhaps it may be possible to eliminate it if leaders of each country could enforce human rights in their country. Implementation of human rights is definitely a huge eradicator of sex trafficking, as the following causes of prostitution and sex trafficking such as poverty, unemployment, lack of education, dejection, sexual abuse, and other forms of struggle are all addressed as human rights issues.

It is difficult to expect morality from troubled souls. However, remember that prostitution is also known as one of the oldest professions in the world. Even though it diminishes souls and destroys lives, people still indulge in this type of sexual activity. One of the main reasons for human trafficking is sex. It is quite common in Eastern Europe, for instance, for women and girls to be sold and bought. Sometimes even boys. There was a system in Germany where prostitution was controlled by the government for the benefit of workers and laborers. The rationale behind this was that it kept the men out of mischief and prevented crimes such as rape.

Prostitution is more or less legal in some European countries where it is not so heavily frowned upon, such as in places like the Netherlands and Scandinavia, where the crime rate is rather low because of the relative freedom that is allotted there. Despite the acceptance of this profession in certain developed countries, I still maintain that it is morally unacceptable and bad for the spiritual development and dignity of all the parties involved.

I see Italians who are very eager to point fingers at the Nigerian, Russian, and South American prostitutes in Italy. I understand their plight, but the patrons of prostitutes are as guilty as the prostitutes themselves and the traffickers, as is the law of supply and demand. If they stop patronizing the prostitutes, that will definitely reduce the crime drastically.

Again, it is an awful way of making a living, but Nigerian prostitutes in Italy are not the only prostitutes in the world. There are prostitutes in every country, and many choose to travel out to other countries to indulge. I have met Italian, Russian, and English prostitutes in America and American prostitutes in Italy and Germany. So, while people sit there and point fingers in criticism, their sister or daughter or female relative or friend may be somewhere in another country selling sex for whatever reason. Yes, there are some prostitutes who do it for fun, some do it to feel loved and wanted because of low self-esteem issues, some do it as a result of relentless abuse during childhood, and some do it for survival.

A patron of prostitutes is also a prostitute of sorts.

The Power of Your Essence

When you can live from your essence, you will be free of hate toward self and toward others and all the evil behavior that burdens the soul and generates more evil and inevitably evokes ill luck.

Learn to walk in a higher frequency, a higher vantage point where there is wholeness and liberty.

Let your worries, when you have any, be focused on the need for harmony in the world and not in the nonsensical that only reveals your inferiority complex and bitterness.

Misunderstanding and Misapplication of Culture

It seems almost impulsive to emulate certain aspects of other cultures—especially those that are appealing or trendy—without questioning or trying to understand their genesis.

Yes, some traditions are akin to trends, as they are appealing to many people and are thus spontaneously adopted as part of a belief system or part of the lifestyle. It never occurs to the emulators that there must be a deeper meaning to the act than meets the eye.

Also, some may provoke confusion in our lives, just because we lack the full understanding and thus misapply them at will.

African children, for instance, are eager to practice some aspects of Western culture, especially the ones that are birthed in prison yards and ghettos.

A major example is the sagging pants. Our children are sagging their pants, because they saw rappers sagging their pants in music videos. However, it is unknown to them that sagging pants originated from the prison yards, and it was used as a secret code to indicate interest in homosexuality to other likeminded inmates. There are so many other such examples.

Bride Price

I think the cultures that practice this custom should be more thoughtful on the price, as not every family seems to be able to afford an enormous bride price, as demanded by tradition when their daughter returns home for whatever reason. Now, some of the major reasons women are eager to leave their marriage are infidelity and abuse. I know that in the old era, or even as recent as a few years ago, women were compelled by tradition to tolerate and endure dreadful behavior from their partners, because divorce is almost like a taboo in their respective cultures, as the woman would automatically lose her respect the moment she walked away from her husband's home, despite the validity of the reasons. In fact, some Nigerian cultures still practice this type of ignorance. Only the youth, the modern children are rebelling against it and hitting the road as soon as necessary without yielding to family warnings or traditions.

Now, why should the bride price be expensive as if selling off daughters and indirectly forcing them to remain in a toxic environment where you cannot reimburse the payments? I hear some parents argue that the reason for such a high bride price is because they spent lavishly on raising and educating their daughters. THEIR daughters! Ridiculous! You need to be paid for taking care of your responsibility? You ought to raise your own offspring and be proud that you are able to do so and not expect payment or expect to reap from their future!

You expect your child to endure abuse in any form just because you want to enjoy some gain from her future? Do you realize that abuse has the propensity of escalating, and death becomes imminent where there is chronic abuse? The woman may continuously endure it but subconsciously grow bitter, which can spiral out of control and translate to violence on her part; in some cases, some women resort to poisoning or other method of disposing of their violent husbands, hence the common paranoia that widows are often responsible for the deaths of their husbands.

Traditions can be interesting if the practices are realistic and healthy and not entailing wicked behavior or ignorance that can escalate into unforeseeable consequences that can be detrimental to a person's life.

Hating on a Giver

Do not hate on someone who is capable and willing to do good deeds for their fellow man just because you are not? That awful reaction already reveals that you are not willing to show kindness and generosity to others even if you indeed possess the means and ability to be of service. It further shows that you lack appreciation for general life and happiness, so you would not grasp the depth and meaning of even making sacrifices for the comfort and safety of others.

Do you know that appreciating someone in the position to do good who does so willingly would lift up your own spirit and also activate success in your life so that you yourself would follow in the noble tradition of selfless service?

Hiding Behind Fake Profiles

It is cowardly and despicable to hide behind fake social networking profiles in order to browse pages of those you scorn or of those who abhor your attitude and personality. Why are you so eager to keep tabs on a person? Is it because you are envious and are losing your mind because the fellow is living their life? Yes, you are green with envy, and that is why you are obsessively racing to the person's domain every day to go through their updates.

Stop torturing yourself and focus on building your own life. You detract from your journey and repress your spirit every time you spend energy on nonsensical obsessions with other people's lives.

Now, there are those of you that wish other people failure, so you race to their wall hiding behind a fake profile to see what is happening. So what if the person is really failing? How does that elevate your miserable life? Yes, I believe you are miserable, because your despicable act reveals depression and failure. Healthy spirits and successful personalities have little or no time for such cheap games. Only losers and weak souls do. In case you are questioning yourself right now, I urge you to reflect on your life to sort your misery out, so that your judgment would be clearer and your decisions inclined to propriety. Be aware that wishing others bad and celebrating their downfall only invokes ill luck upon your life. Your miserable existence will never ever get better because someone else did not succeed!

The really miserable ones are those that wish your downfall and peddle malicious gossip around the networks to smear your reputation. But then, unfortunately for them, you are succeeding. Your life is propelling upward, and they see it each time they peer at your profile. And the more they see positivity in your life, the more unhappy and angry they become. Wow! The devil delights in such intensity of anger and frustration and exploits that anger to destroy the recipients' lives, thus causing the emission of only dark clouds and no light on their path.

Just because you hate someone and wish them death or failure does not necessarily mean that those wishes will manifest. You will never ever be that person's God, nor do you have the power to dictate the person's destiny. So be realistic about what you do against your victims and your expectations thereafter. In fact, it would be more rewarding for you to wish your enemies good, and by doing so, avoid invoking a burden upon your soul.

Do you realize that you are also a victim to your victims? Yes, reversed psychological control. They have governance over you from a distance, because they occupy your mind and dictate your actions, driving you to do and wish harm against them, seeking their failure, an act that can eventually lead to your own destruction. Oh yes, darling, the spirit of hate, envy, wickedness, and malicious gossip are all a huge burden unto the soul and detrimental to one's life and growth.

So I ask you, is this person's downfall worth you colliding with misery as well? Something to ponder on!

Perhaps, you need to be a little more thoughtful for your own good. The act of thinking reveals important factors and grants us a better insight to situations and goals. Though in this case, it is an evil goal, it still needs very deep and careful thinking.

Parents' Perception of Their Children

Parents, it is impossible for all your children to possess the same attributes as you. Each one of us is an individual with different chromosomes. No two people are exactly the same, even identical twins. Our behavior and perception of life are a part of our journey to realizing our purpose as individuals. Your duty as a parent is to raise and guide them to be good citizens so that they can have a solid foundation upon which they can structure and balance their lives.

For example, there is the stubborn behavior which often has its own distinct purpose. Leaders, for instance, are usually better off possessing an aggressive spirit to prevent the ignorant from trampling over them and impeding their success. A rebellious spirit can also become an impediment where there is a lack of wisdom, hence the need for a spiritual foundation.

Even the meek children must be guided and watched, else they would collide with very difficult challenges that will repress them, as we live in a world permeated by wicked spirits who are eager to manipulate the meek. In fact, meekness can be misconstrued as weakness, which makes balance necessary.

Every attribute we possess as individuals is a tool to realizing our purpose, but we must seek structure and balance and then pursue our purpose.

The Subjugation of Women

It is said that African men, for example, believe in the subjugation of women. That is an attitude you will witness often in that part of the world without any form of disguise or pretense. It is considered natural. When a bold, independent, beautiful young woman decides to step out into the male world looking to advance herself in any chosen path and seeks help or support from those in control of the system—mostly men—she is immediately impeded. Unless, of course, she dances to their tune. The tune is almost always sexual. She must give up her body before, during, or after they have rendered their assistance.

No matter how mind-blowing, brilliant, and useful the innovation is, priorities change instantly when feminine attractiveness is brought to bear down on them. The more powerful and influential the man, the more likely he is to resort to bribery or even blackmail. It could be mild and subtle or obvious and persistent, but the motive is almost always the same. To "get into the woman's panties!"

Sometimes, men in certain parts of Nigeria, for example, insist on subjugating the woman by ensuring she "stays in her place," so to speak, by making sure she does not "rise above her station." They think she is only entitled to be someone's wife and/or mother. Educational facilities and job opportunities are usually blocked from the female. Right from infancy in some parts of the country, the girl child is forbidden to participate in formal education that may end up putting her on par with men. In other parts of the country, women are denied property rights.

However, the saddest part of it all, as I said earlier, is that well-educated men of substance and power cannot control their indulgence in women and feel it is their right to bed all the pretty and not-so-pretty ones.

Whenever they set eyes on the excessively beautiful, they become aggressive and determined and will spend any amount of money or grant any favor to get their way. It works for them most of the time. A lot of women feel they have no choice but to compromise, which in itself makes it more difficult for the very strong minority to gain respect, because most men find it hard to accept rejection and will not hesitate to shut the door to any opportunity offered once they are convinced the woman is unlikely to submit herself.

There is absolutely nothing wrong with being a red-blooded male naturally attracted to a gorgeous woman, but one must maintain one's posture as a gentleman, remain disciplined, exude confidence and self-control, and be chivalrous and attentive to the needs of the woman he desires for as long as it takes, then she in turn will grow to love and respect him and eventually the union of two consenting adults will be blessed.

May God forgive the weak men for their inferior personalities and help them to become real gentlemen, and may He also grant the weak women the courage and strength to take better care of themselves!

There's Real Security in Self-Reliance!

We are all subject to challenges, and only some of us have the willpower to rise above our struggles. Some of us also have people willing and able to aid us through those challenges, which can alleviate the pain and suffering resulting from them.

It is certainly easier to confront and deal with some challenges when one gains support of some sort; however, that also depends on the type of challenge and its magnitude. Your aides and friends may not always be able to support you during challenges, but that should not deter your fight for victory. Remember, they are also humans with weaknesses and strengths just like you; they may have their own aspirations and difficulties, so sometimes, you may collide with problems at the same time they are confronted with challenges. Their own individual challenges that need to be addressed too. Thus, they may have to channel their focus and energy on seeking solutions for their challenges instead of running to your aid. Now, that does not mean they are awful friends or people, neither should it undermine the past aid offered to you.

Do not get accustomed to people supporting you and do not place all your confidence in such people, as that is a shortcut to making yourself a victim. If you depend on other people, you may be devoid of the real security of self-reliance, and you could thus be heading toward an intense pitfall.

Do You Sacrifice Your Happiness and Comfort to Help Others?

Making such a noble sacrifice to support others is supposed to be appreciated and gain one respect accordingly, but unfortunately, we live in a world permeated by ignorant and wicked souls who would rather trample and exploit those eager to make extreme sacrifices to help them. They misconstrue kindness for weakness and are swift to justify their actions when they are rebuked or when they deem it necessary to do so. In fact, they feel entitled to the sacrifices you make, just because you are a friend or sibling . . . Ridiculous! Just because you are my friend or sibling does not earn you my blood. Rather, it is a privilege not an obligation for a friend or sibling to make any kind of sacrifice for you.

I, for instance, have been through countless stages in my life where I sacrificed my happiness and comfort to aid those in need and those who pretended to be in need because of covetousness. In the end, I realized I was dealing with ingrates, people that lack appreciation for compassion and who therefore do not deserve compassion. It was difficult for me to understand that harsh realization, but I eventually had to accept, learn the lessons therein, and move on.

One thing I have to say, though, is that I never stopped being kind and generous. I am still sacrificing my happiness and comfort even now to help others, but it is on another level and with a greater awareness of the reasons and the dangers out there. Most importantly, it is now done within the journey to my destiny. I now choose friends and family members to sacrifice for, without obligation but with pleasure. I choose to yield to my calling to be a voice, even though it is extremely demanding and sometimes causes discomfort and sorrow for me when I meet with the children in pain and with the inferior leaders who are destroying our nation and exploiting our youths, even though I know that it provokes jealousy and hatred in those who cannot fathom the glory of God upon my life. You cannot change from being the quality soul you are because wicked spirits do not appreciate you! However, you can decide who you sacrifice for, as long as it is part of the journey to your destiny.

Whatever the case may be, you always need the guidance of the Holy Spirit and the Grace of God. May God grant us peace, courage, knowledge, and wisdom to deal with people!

Greed in High Places

Government officials are expected to serve the people, but most of them would rather exploit and abuse the people, thereby destroying the nation's integrity at will.

What I really do not understand is how a country like Nigeria can be so wealthy, yet the people live in abject poverty. How can these criminals in government even claim intelligence when they steal from themselves and enrich another man's land? Yes, take Switzerland for instance. It is a little country with almost no natural resources that lives mainly on banking. And yet, it is a little paradise and is so rich, because criminals such as government officials in Nigeria loot the country and whisk it out to Switzerland. How smart are you when you embezzle your country to enrich another man's land? And then, of course, as soon as you are out of government or in trouble, they seize the money. It is only lately that money laundering laws have made it difficult for Switzerland to benefit much.

It defies rationale to understand why a single man would make himself as rich as a country. Some individuals in the country are so wealthy, yet they are not even acknowledged by international statistics such as *Forbes*, because the wealth is ill-gotten. The so-called richest man in Africa has other African people who are much richer than him but are not mentioned, because they were military rulers and dictators who looted the country of money they cannot account for or spend in their lifetime, while those around them are suffering. The oil rich states are a brilliant example of when a few looters or financial marauders descend on the oil wealth to the detriment of the local indigenes. They usually do not try to compensate the people. Their greed and selfishness is immense and unprecedented.

Almost 25 percent of the African population is of Nigerian descent. The land is among the richest in the world. There is nothing really lacking. Take human resources for example—in fact, we have a very young population up to 60 percent, a population that could even build a country if they were well guided. We have mineral and agricultural resources that we have been ignoring of late because of the get-rich-quick wealth of oil.

There was a time we even ignored gas, which is as lucrative as oil, because we were so ignorant that we thought only of oil! Oil! Oil! We were burning away another valuable resource, such as gas, without even contemplating how to cap and refine the damn thing! For example, you go out into certain parts of the rural areas, and you see all kinds of fruits and nuts such as cashew nuts, avocados, and mangoes rotting on the ground. Tons of this stuff is left to go bad, because there is only so much that individuals can consume, and they grow in such excess that they are left to decay. It never occurred to the natives—or better still, no one has taught them—that these are industries they could specialize in and develop that would sustain them and bring up their standard of living if these things are grown and nurtured with care, refined, packaged and sold, even exported.

We sit back like lazy idiots and allow Malaysian people to buy palm kernels from us which were also left to rot in the ground. They take it away, back to their own land, where they have a fraction of what we have by way of agriculture produce, and they painstakingly study its benefits to grow, refine, and manufacture the oil. Soon, lo and behold, they become the biggest palm oil exporters in the world. They simply refined the product and sold it back to us and to many other countries, and we stupidly bought from them what we are sitting on and watching rot in our own backyard!

We were even the largest chocolate producer in the world, mostly in the South-West, with all its cocoa, but what has happened to our cocoa plantations? Ghana has taken over that. They produce and export cocoa to other countries and make chocolate more than Nigeria, which was once the largest cocoa producer in the world during the British colonial days. And what happened to the groundnut pyramids in the northern part of the region? They are no longer there. Again, Nigeria was and probably still is the largest groundnut producer in the world. All the peanuts all over the place originated from this part of West Africa. What is going on? Why can we not resuscitate everything and stop just focusing on oil?

There are corn fields everywhere. Imagine the fact that there are states in Nigeria that are wealthy in semiprecious stones; notwithstanding the fact that we do have gold and silver, but we also have excess of semiprecious stones.

Leather from snake skins to cow hides, we just slaughter the animals and eat them. We do not even have to kill giant snakes or pythons or boas to get hold of their skin to make shoes and bags—they molt and leave their skin all over their territory, so we can get those and produce beautiful shoes and purses.

The locals just pick them up and make slippers and bags, and they are done in such a lackadaisical manner, with no vision to build a more lucrative industry for leather goods.

The list continues.

Men, You Can Provoke The Nagging

Yes, a man can provoke his woman to nag by his attitude and behavior toward her and the relationship, even though nagging is never the solution and is rather detrimental. Now, if you are disloyal or abusive, then most definitely you would create a monster in your woman. I do not think a woman with a healthy spirit would naturally want to nag at her man unless she is provoked to do so. However, there are a few other reasons why a woman nags that are not really the man's fault. In fact, these reasons also apply to nagging men. A woman or man with low self-esteem is likely to provoke your doubt about your mate's loyalty to you and the relationship. Naturally, the low estimation of self can cause self-deprecation, which instigates negative imaginations in the mind about other people's perception of you and in fact even their attitude toward you would be questioned and analyzed and judged in a distorted manner.

Then, you begin to believe that your mate and others may even regard you lower than you estimated yourself, and you instinctively nurture these thoughts, and they unconsciously start to influence your actions and thereby provoke the nagging attitude and other awful behavior.

More Causes of Nagging

Control is also the cause for nagging. When one person feels the need to control another, they tend to nag at every little thing and with every little opportunity. Such personalities believe they exercise power or establish authority by nagging. Ridiculous! And the need to control is usually provoked by low self-esteem. Yes, people with self-esteem issues use control to mask their inferiority complex or as a tool to elevate themselves and to provoke fear in their mate or those in their vicinity.

Gossip is also another cause of a woman's nagging attitude. Most women who are approached with stories about their partners cannot resist listening to them. They almost always give audience to malicious gossip involving their mates, even though they are not sure of the talebearer's motives. Subsequently, they eagerly nag at their mate even without proof that he is guilty.

However, all of these traits can be discernible to an alert mind, one that also possesses wisdom and a good grasp of relationship challenges. Be careful not to nag your partner away into another person's arms! May God grant us the peace and wisdom to deal with our relationship issues.

YOUR IDENTITY

Who are you? Do you know who you are? It is unfortunate that many of us lack the knowledge of self and rather hide under the shadow of wealthy parents or famous relatives or rich partners or friends.

No, you are not to be truly revered because of these shadows, and you would not be identified by any of them either. Discover yourself, catch your own vision, try to create your own goals, and pursue them to the best of your capabilities so that when you realize them, you can give significance to your existence and command your own respect. May God rekindle the greatness within you.

People Around Government Officials Who Extort Money From Others to Make Introductions

Corrupt practices in this instance start with the security guard who wants to be bribed to even let you into the building. He usually claims to have a close relationship with the politician or senior executive and can facilitate your business with the "boss," if you can entice him with some money. Thereafter, try the Special Advisors or ADCs and even the Personal Assistants. What about the so-called Media Coordinators and all sorts of Assistants and Secretaries? Everyone is eager and desperate to extort money from you or impede your business with their boss if you do not cooperate. There is also the "missing file syndrome" which would reappear quickly if financial interests are taken care of. All these hitches happen regardless of the interest of their boss.

Don't try doing any kind of business with a politician or Chief Executive where there is a middle-person who would even add more money to the proposals in order to get their cut, then collect the funds and not pay you. It is hard enough to get paid by the person you are dealing with, as they can sometimes be very selfish individuals who believe they are gods and care less about people they do deals with. Thus, they treat affairs with them nonchalantly. They observe a society pervaded with people floored by poverty, and so they are devoid of principles and human feelings. Otherwise, one can keep on wondering why corruption is so embedded at all levels within the system.

But those of you who encounter these despicable personalities should not be discouraged from your goals, as they are only another challenge that you must also confront and conquer. Where it proves formidable, seek help or device another strategy to pursue and achieve your honorable business intentions.

May God grant you the courage and patience to confront these challenges.

The World is My Oyster

I am striving for growth
The goal is to attain my full potential

I will explore every opportunity available to me
My significance in life depends on my contribution to humanity

My flaws are trivial to my great qualities
My dominant gift is in my boldness and ability to illuminate others' path

My generation is taking a plunge into darkness
My efforts will enforce the strength of like-minded spirits and together we will eradicate darkness

The wonders of life gravitate to me
Agents of darkness are my footstool

My spirit is on the quest to conquer pain and sorrow
I am a conqueror

I am a global phenomenon
I am a child of destiny

SEPTEMBER 11—GREAT AMERICA

The memory of a sorrowful event is not to rekindle your pain but to compel a focus on healing, to encourage a forge on, as well as celebrate the strength of the nation thus far.

September 11 is indeed a sorrowful event that must not rule our souls and depress us but strengthen us. I plead the peace and grace of God upon the life of every American and every other nationality that suffered losses and ask that God pacify and strengthen the family members of the victims. I love you, America, and I thank you and God for my strength.

POVERTY OF THE SPIRIT

Financial poverty is not the only cause of greed, selfishness, extortion, and exploitation, because even some successful people and politicians in Nigeria and other societies across the globe still exhibit the same behavior as the poverty-stricken people. They are probably greedier and more selfish and are eager to exploit and manipulate the vulnerable for financial gain than the poor people.

Poverty of spirit is the reason for such despicable and repulsive behavior. Yes, it may even start from financial poverty and degenerate into spiritual poverty. Poverty of the spirit can be inherent. If you are born into a family with the spirit of poverty, then you're most likely going to possess the spirit of poverty as well, unless you discover the word of God and heal yourself.

No more speculating why rich or educated or seemingly honorable men and women and politicians will be greedy, eager to extort money, refuse to pay their debt, or pay those who work for or with them. No more wondering about the reason your loved ones and so-called friends will cheat you for money or will refuse to pay money due to you. It is rooted in the spirit. It is poverty of the spirit! They do the stealing, exploitation, and extortion so unabashedly, as if it is acceptable.

May God release you from poverty of spirit and also grant the victims the grace and peace to deal with their situations!

Celebrating Your Parents

I thank God for the life and the gifts of my mother and father. So many people out there have lost either one or both of their parents, and some even look on with a slight pang of envy and /or longing when they encounter friends and acquaintances communicating with and appreciating their parent(s).

These are, if you like, the twilight years of most of our parents' generation, a period when we should be caring for them and enjoying every precious moment we can with them, because as we all know, life is transient!

Celebrate your time with them, especially birthdays, anniversaries, etc., like your whole life depended on it and relish the joy you bring into their lives and the look of contentment on their faces. Treasure each memorable moment you can with them and continue to learn from them bits of the history of your life and origins that are vague or nonexistent in your recollection. These are times of your growth that will always be a legacy in your mental archives to be passed on to your offspring for their own enlightenment and eventual onward transmission to their own children and so on for all eternity.

Remember, we wouldn't be here if it were not for them. No matter how you look at it, God nominated them to be our guardians for his greater plans, and usually, what a great job they managed to do in spring-boarding us to this point in our lives. May God grant us the courage and wisdom to celebrate our parents.

FORTY-FOUR YEARS OF MARRIAGE AND LIVING IN HARMONY, my mum and dad.

Wardrobes and Image

You must not emulate every lifestyle you watch on television or every experience with a celebrity or a public image, because it is not necessarily for you to adopt. That style is a component of their image, a part of the package that is created to distinguish and sell the brand. Because a celebrity wears it does not mean it is right for you. There are consequences for the certain wardrobe one wears when one is in the wrong environment, so this must be a real factor for consideration.

It is interesting to see African women wear micro and miniskirts or booty shorts in Africa when it is deemed wrong in our culture and in addition the system is not structured to protect them when they are sexually harassed, which is likely to occur with such wardrobe.

It is not that miniskirts are entirely wrong, but in some societies like those without law and order, where men tend to act like animals on impulse and believe women are for abuse and use, it is an invitation for rape. It provokes verbal abuse in a culture where the women are expected to cover up as well. However, these customary laws do not apply to an artist who is there to entertain and stimulate you. Therefore, people must expect the artist to style differently.

CHOICE

Your choice can be determined by your purpose, grasp of the objective, conditions attached, level of aspiration, strength, or willpower etc., while your agony can be caused by the wrong objective, wrong approach, circumstances attached, grasp of the objective, level of focus, level of aspiration, mental and emotional state, limitations, and even ignorance, hence the need to ponder deeply on one's goals and all that it entails to pursue them.

Act of Thinking

When you think of something, you give it life, because the act of thinking is an infusion of energy into the very idea you have conceived or are nurturing.

The act of thinking is a compelled focus on the idea or subject one is analyzing or dissecting. Thinking also allows the mind to conceive new ideas.

Thinking can be impossible when the mind is plunged into depression; thus, tranquility is essential for forming thoughts.

A stifled spirit is depleted of in-depth thinking and rather inclined to negative thoughts, as one's judgment becomes distorted. Impulsive actions and reactions are devoid of thoughts and rationality.

ALTERNATIVE

Having an alternative influences one's judgments in the subconscious, because if you were depleted of choice, you are likely to try to rationalize the situation, so you will be more patient, focused, calculated, considerate, tolerant, thoughtful, etc., and all of these actions can give you other perspectives to the situation and can aide in achieving the desired goal.

So instead of thinking of an "alternative," focus and invest your all on your objective.

A Toxic Environment is Extensively Destructive

Yes, a toxic environment could have a strong negative effect on every facet of your life, from your career to your interactions with people, to your business transactions, and even friendships. Of course, violent behavior of your mate or siblings or children can cause an emotional crisis, which will definitely affect other facets of your life, as emotion plays a major role in every aspect of our lives.

A toxic environment includes not only violence but poverty and inhuman conditions such as unhygienic and filthy neighborhoods riddled with rodents and cockroaches, deprivation, illiteracy, ignorance, superstition, and crime.

Some of the social crises we experience in society are the results of people dwelling in a toxic environment.

The worst type of toxic environment could be those created by war type situations where there is starvation, hatred, destruction, and death.

So how do we get out of toxic environments, then? I think if you love yourself, you will get out of it and find yourself heading toward a healthy place once you start boosting your self-esteem in spite of your flaws, failure, negative utterances about you, etc., if you can convince yourself to not be afraid of these things then you will want to live a healthy life and dwell in a healthy environment.

Usually, our wants and desires influence our decisions and actions. Thus, our needs toward ourselves will be reflected positively once we are aware of what we want and what is good for us.

MAKE-BELIEVE

Make-believe is as effective as the reality, because expressing the right emotions at the right times can also stimulate one's objective by feeling the desired emotions you would feel from imagining the experience you want to create. However, make-believe is devoid of morality and substance.

May God guide us through the right path to achieving our good desires.

Blind Comparison

If you are single, focus on being a better you instead of looking for who is better than your ex.

If you improve yourself, you are likely to attract a more suitable mate who is better than your ex.

Be aware that everyone has some type of flaw, and what makes a person ideal for you as an individual is your ability to understand and tolerate the fellow's shortcomings and vice versa. That is a very important decisive factor.

Being you, good or bad, could also inspire the personality you experience in your ex. How so? Do you know that even being a good person can provoke evil? Yes, though it is usually in a polluted soul, a spiritually damaged person, even mentally disturbed, someone who has clearly been damaged by a toxic environment. Such toxic environments encourage people to doubt and antagonize good personalities. Polluted environments also promote the belief that abuse is a natural extension of a relationship or that one must be violent to establish authority or power. Some even go as far as claiming that physical abuse based on jealousy, discipline, and control is a sign that the abuser loves and cares for the abused!

Be careful not to hamper your happiness by your idealistic fantasies or by searching for a better mate in unrealistic ways (i.e., always comparing new loves to the former). Yes, your judgment may be clouded by your desperation, thereby ensnaring you into a worse relationship. Just focus on your personal growth and understand more about yourself and managing relationships, as these two factors will help in attracting your ideal mate and living in harmony with them.

Defensive Approach

I have learned that people get very defensive and race to war when their evil intentions are questioned. Those evil intentions may not even be apparent, but a person asking a simple or fundamental question will provoke an internal crisis in the wicked. That is because the wicked believe they are superior and in control, hence the conception and reaction of evil in their mind and the masterminded strategy to pursue those evil intentions.

What Happens When You Wake Up One Day And You Are No Longer In Charge?

Yes, most people—especially men—decline in spirit when they fall from grace or are depleted of their financial wealth, thus stripping them of their authority or the type of power gained through financial wealth.

In my opinion, confidence and power should be based in the spirit, not in status and financial wealth, even though achievements do elevate one's self-esteem. So for instance, if one is relegated in status and/or is destitute and is naturally diminished in spirit, one could rise up again quickly, because the source of power comes from one's spirit.

Do you know that spiritual wealth, which is the genesis of real solid power, actually attracts financial success and can elevate one's status? The Holy Spirit can infuse one with spiritual wealth, as that encompasses one's flaws and strength, and very few can develop a healthy self-esteem with all the mistakes and flaws and failure that can demoralize most people.

Purge Your Environment

It is important to purge your environment of the wrong habits and people as soon as you realize which of the occupants are toxic. Endless unproductive activities, arguments, complaints, sulking, and whining are only going to diminish your spirit and, in fact, cause you more problems. You even stifle other people's spirit by your constant complaining. Do you know that even the people outside your immediate world could also be affected by the consequences of your polluted immediate world? Yes, your irritated spirit is out there interacting with people, and there is a tendency for you to have negative, contrived judgments of actions and deeds by others.

We must be careful how we carry out what transpires in our immediate world to the outside world and also how we bring home what transpires in the outside world, for there are inevitable consequences. The solution would be to cleanse your infected environment and refurnish it with peace again, so that your dispositions are healthy and appealing. Believe me, a polluted environment is repelling to happiness and absolutely depleted of everything that can propel success. It is indeed an awful experience. Flush out your environment and see how new and refreshing even the air you breathe becomes. Your energy experiences a swift boost, and perspectives are suddenly clear in the conceptions of your ideas.

Imagine spending your day trying hard to please people who just cannot be pleased in spite of your efforts. Imagine waking up to angry spirits. Imagine dealing with people whose journey is not in alignment with yours, so they make it difficult to coexist in your environment. Imagine people who constantly criticize you or look for reasons to cut you down. Imagine interacting with people who lack the full appreciation for who you are and what you do. Imagine people with no real ambition who are rather busy peddling malicious gossip about you. Imagine people who are not remorseful of their evil actions toward you and are rather eager to project their guilt unto you.

Purge your environment of these pollutions in order for your life to flourish. Do not let them drag you down!

Govern What Transpires in Your World

You must learn to govern what transpires in your immediate world. You are responsible for the condition of your immediate world, whether good or bad. It is important to know that your immediate world would, to a certain point, extend to your outside world, though it may be gradual and indirect. The people you confide in, live with, or interact with regularly can enrich or pollute your world. I know that sometimes we want to believe we have a good grasp of a person's character and are capable of understanding personalities. We also tend to read positive meaning into their smile and fun conversations and little favors, which should be healthy for the spirit and for the growth of the relationship. However, these qualities are predisposed to change and may also be pretentious for selfish reasons unknown to us. People almost always wear masks for different reasons. Yes, we all wear different masks, consciously and unconsciously, due to the harshness and complexities of life that make us feel the need to protect our true selves.

So how then can one choose the people, the personalities, suitable for one's immediate world without making wrong choices?

Some people are also adept at immersing themselves into a personality that is rewarding for as long as it takes, so you may be dealing with dual or multiple personalities, and your judgment of that particular person's dispositions are thus likely to be wrong. Ugh!

In my opinion, it is wise to be open to people. However, judge carefully, and when in doubt, ask for guidance.

The Weak Associates

Betrayers, rats, backstabbers . . . There are coworkers or friends who would pretend or even claim to be in accord with your good intentions and principles, but as soon as they find themselves in an awkward position, their mental strength challenged or confronted by the boss and perhaps a soulless lad eager to repress, manipulate, and exploit employees and coworkers, they would snitch or even oppose those same good intentions and principles you have. These types of associates are weak, vicious, and lacking in wisdom and are often prone to be the devil's prey.

The colleague may also be compelled by personal circumstances to turn against you, such as if your colleague is receiving favors from or is reliant on your boss for living support etc.

Therefore, be careful how you disclose your plans to your colleagues, in spite of the impressions they may give of themselves, unless they have earned your trust over time and through events that have shown you their character.

The Power of Gratitude

Gratitude inspires more gain and positivity. When the heart is grateful for its attainment, it automatically unleashes the power of light and creates room for more achievements.

A happy spirit is inclined to clear and positive thinking which reflects good judgment and propels success and the good life.

Showing gratitude to those who are benevolent toward you can delight their soul and inspire them to favor you even the more.

There is something very dark and ugly about discontentment and ingratitude. First, it reflects weakness of spirit, because a true, potent spirit appreciates achievements and favors. A weak spirit is an unattractive spirit and a vulnerable spirit. Thus, we must endeavor to heal and strengthen our spirit when we are weak. Ingratitude provokes the spirit of anger and perhaps pain in those that are worthy of our thankfulness, hence the aforementioned darkness and ugliness. The spirit of ingratitude is a repellent to success and happiness and must be purged immediately to unleash light!

CYBER PREYING MANTIS

A large number of people on Facebook and social media refuse to act within the realms of propriety simply because they are miserable in their own little world and feel the desperate need to peddle their misery on other people's walls. To those of you who fall victim to these weak personalities, why waste your time and energy getting angry over such trivialities? Do you know that your reaction to or perception of a person and their deed gives significance to them? In other words, you can choose not to acknowledge them by ignoring what they say and taking steps to delete or block them so they do not have access to peddle their follies in your domain.

YOUR ATTITUDE

Struggles and challenges tend to alter a positive mindset into that of a very bad attitude. However, it is critical to understand that a bad attitude can only generate more negativity and cause you even bigger challenges. A negative outlook causes many human problems, although it is not obvious to a burdened mind. It reflects weakness of spirit and low self-esteem.

A bad attitude cannot always be concealed, even if masking may be required in certain situations for easy interaction and progression, because negativity has the propensity to pollute the conscious mind where thoughts are generated. The cosmetic fix cannot remain fresh all day. It will definitely wear off and requires you to touch up. If you are not conscious of touching up your make-up, the real person will be revealed. And you cannot always be mindful of touching up. Hence the saying, "You can fool some people sometime, but you can't fool all the people all of the time."

In addition, life has a way of peeling or cracking our masks, no matter what material they are made of. Therefore, it is healthier to make an effort toward changing your negative views of life so that you can flourish and live life to your full potential.

The Employer

You may believe that the well-being of your employees is not your responsibility, but it really becomes your responsibility to a certain level from the inception of their employment, at least during the hours they are offering their services to you, and it is only gracious and good business to concern yourself to a reasonable degree about those who are working for you.

Quality Company

Keeping quality company has a positive influence in your life. In addition to drawing your inspirations from these quality friends and family members, they can attract good energy to you because of their good spirit and pure love toward you, and they are also quick on their feet when you find yourself in crises beyond your own control. They could even make investments toward your progress, because they appreciate your good soul and your talents and believe in your future.

Have you noticed that family members and friends of questionable quality would watch you suffer (even withhold debts owed to you, especially if they find out you need it), would never sacrifice to help you, and would in fact seek your downfall or try to impede your progress at any given chance? They are eager to smear your reputation, condemn you at any slightest opportunity, race to deplete you of all you have if you let them, and never support your dreams and goals, even if they may pretend to.

Even indulging in a "mere" phone conversation, like many would see it, should be done with quality souls. We are all spirits, and one must try to steer clear of those spirits that are not in alignment with one's spirit and those souls that are wallowing in failure and anger to avoid polluting one's soul. There is also a strong energy one exudes when speaking, so that energy may be carrying a spirit that conflicts with yours. Yes, someone can pollute your spirit if their spirit is toxic or impure or even hypocritical toward you. People can deposit evil in your spirit or provoke crisis in your life just by uttering one ill word. The conversation may also be about another person other than you and may still consist of evil that would unconsciously contaminate your life, hence the need to only indulge quality people on the phone as well.

You may just be lounging in your house with your family and maybe friends, or you may just be catching up on your rest, when suddenly a not so quality sibling, colleague, associate, or friend calls with some negative stories or gossip and contaminates your spirit. Stay away from them!

MANIPULATING THE MIND

In order to manipulate the mind, you have to fascinate it, and the only way to intrigue the mind for exploitation is to feed it with the information that is alluring and new or that seems to be a pathway to progress or reward desirable to the subject. Inferior leaders are usually eager to lure and exploit available minds to achieve their own selfish needs. They make you believe they care about you, but they really do not, because their interest is with themselves and not you.

May God help us to identify these types of leaders and grant us the courage to steer clear from them!

Doubting Your Mate

When you begin to doubt your mate's loyalty to you or notice awkward behavior that provokes doubt, it is imperative to approach your mate with your concerns, and you must do so politely.

Communication is a major tool in a healthy relationship, and couples must try to communicate with each other, regardless of what the issues are. Being intrusive in your mate's privacy probing for answers is not a healthy option and would only compound your problems.

You may also be fostering a wrong instinct. What are you trying to accomplish? First of all, a relationship without trust is depleted of longevity and is especially yielding to failure when you cultivate the habit of invading your partner's privacy. You will be seeking trouble. The only things you would achieve by such awful behavior is to cause yourself a heartache and compound your problems or widen the void between the both of you.

Your Sick Spouse

A "wedding band" is not just a marriage band but a virtue that must be embraced and practiced in marriage, so if your mate is sick, for instance, you have to be a vessel for their healing process.

Do you know that a peaceful environment is a vital element of healing for a sick person? Your compassion, love, and care collectively inspires and promotes a peaceful environment, and you must therefore do everything necessary to ensure peace around your ailing spouse. I know that sometimes a sick person can do things that are irritating or provoking to those who love them and thereby engender friction, but you have to understand that such behavior is not intentional but an element or consequence of their weakened spirit.

You can never understand the depth of the trauma they suffer, so if you must cast criticisms, always do so with compassion. Remember, if you were in that position, you would expect your mate to stick by you and nurture you back to health. After all, no one plans to be sick! Affliction is never part of one's future vision or a desire, but anyone could be victimized, regardless of one's aesthetic looks, physical strength, or financial status.

Be careful of the opinions you cultivate toward sick people. It may be your turn tomorrow!

Angry Over Trivialities

Why would you want to burden your soul with anger for something nonsensical? You magnify trivialities, because you are at war within and are thereby unconsciously seeking outlets to express or release the anger that is consuming your weak soul. Be careful, because the spirit of anger can be extensively disastrous, and you most probably cannot undo most detriments that result from anger.

Life Can Be Unfair

It is unfortunate that life does not always serve you or your heart's desires, and even if you do hard labor, you are not always fairly rewarded for it. And then, once in a while, you cross paths with someone who has no talent, lazes around, and deserves little but still gains so much. So then you ask yourself, why you? You, who deserves success, gets so little. The intricacies of life! Okay, then you are told that you have to live on hope, because that is what fuels your life, otherwise you are dead.

Hope? Yes, hope! It sounds silly, as the fact remains that you did work hard, and you explored your talents, yet you were not really rewarded, so now are you supposed to live on hope? But then again, you cannot succeed on just hope. Instead, you need to try to conceive new ideas, pursue new goals, and learn all you can so you know that you are on the right track and then persist and persevere until you achieve success.

My darling, this is all part of the complexities of life, and we must carry on with learning and working until we attain the heights we seek in life. What is that goal you seek?

In my opinion, the ultimate goal you should seek is to realize your purpose in life, so you can develop and use your talents and abilities to be all you can be for yourself and others, which gives significance and meaning to your existence.

Fulfilling Leadership Qualities

There are leaders who have a full grasp of the significance of the position they possess, understanding that selfless service is paramount in leadership and does not place oneself above national interest, though we do not even acknowledge the efforts some of our leaders make to build the nation.

There is a moral virtue that we must learn to adopt, and that is the virtue of appreciation. It is unfortunate that this is not a culture that promotes gratitude, and gratitude is an encouragement to the selfless service we expect from our leaders.

Yes, if you appreciate someone's good works, then the person would be encouraged to do more.

Encourage and support our leaders by highlighting their strengths and minimizing any emphasis on their weaknesses unless it is for constructive purposes. Constant criticism only compounds the problems we are facing. You cannot malign me in spite of my hard work and then expect me to do well by you.

Nigerians, for instance, have this terrible habit of sitting around complaining about their leaders. Yes, they are adept at criticizing and peddling malicious gossip about leaders who they deem incompetent for whatever reason. Everyone appears to be an expert on the faults of the country, and it is true that some of these leaders are indeed guilty. Nonetheless, we need to understand that the government also needs the support of the people in order to be able to serve them better, and the government is the people. We need to understand that today's citizen is tomorrow's leader. An awful citizen makes an incompetent leader, but a patriotic citizen makes a competent and just leader. We must all take responsibility to build our nation. The people must synergize with the government to build the nation. There is power in synergy!

It is not too much to keep reminding our leaders of the full meaning of leadership, a position that epitomizes vision and inspiration. We must do away with mediocrity and focus on true leadership and stick to practicing the principle of using wisdom to guide, protect, and provide comfort and happiness for people.

Communication is also a major factor in effective leadership, but I notice a great lack of communication between government and the people. Plans should be shared with the people being served, and the journey to realization should be traveled together in order to realize a vision.

Oil is Not Everything

Today, we believe, and it is indeed true that colonial Britain exploited our resources to their own economic advantage. Yet, oil was only discovered in commercial quantity in 1956 (four years before Independence). Of course, the Nigerian economy was not without oil during the colonial era, but it was not crude oil. Nigeria at least fared well with palm oil and groundnut oil.

Even at Independence in 1960, the economy was young but strong, virile, and promising. Again, its strength was not oil-based. The discovery of large deposits of crude oil in the Niger-Delta has brought some blessings and boost to our economic fortunes. The total dependence on it will, however, remain the height of economic indiscretion.

So, Nigeria can do without oil; or at most, make oil just one variable of a vast economy. Gas flaring and oil spillage should be stopped to allow fishing and other farming activities to flourish as before in the South-south. There is also iron ore, bitumen, and uranium in the South-south. Bitumen alone as a mineral has a promise of $10 billion to the nation's economy.

The South-east was known for its various palm plantations, rice fields, and many other agricultural products. It also has large deposits of coal, limestone, lead, and zinc ore.

In the South-west, cocoa production could still be restored even beyond its Awolowo days. Other minerals include gold, bitumen, and tantalite.

There are vast agricultural opportunities in the North-central, ranging from varieties of fruit, cassava, rice, etc. It boasts of bauxite, tantalite, iron ore, tin, uranium, and limestone.

In the North-east, we have the millet, maize, fishing opportunities, cattle ranching, etc. Mineral resources in the North-east include uranium, limestone, tin, and niobium.

Finally, the North-west can still rebuild its groundnut pyramids and increase sugar cane production and general agricultural activities. The North-west is also rich in uranium, tin, niobium, gold, soda ash, silica, and gemstone.

All these agricultural and mineral resources have vast and very elastic economic transformational capabilities in the form of industries, foreign investment, export, and general trade.

What to Do in A Chaotic Polygamous Family

I know there are those of you from polygamous families that claim to be in support of polygamy, because you are probably living in peace with your half-siblings and stepmothers, which is great. Or you are enjoying the chaos polygamy may be bringing, which is usually unpleasant. There are also those struggling for peace and harmony every day because of their stepsiblings' and stepparents' acrimonious attitude.

Parents are expected to consider their children in the best light during a bitter divorce, but this is not about a bitter divorce but the struggle of coexisting with antagonistic half-siblings and stepparents.

It is indeed a very sensitive situation, as you are now dealing with family. It is usually easier to confront situations with strangers and friends than it is to deal with family. How then will you deal with hostile stepsiblings and stepmothers?

In my opinion, you should first move away from the toxic environment if possible, as decisions taken there are typically devoid of logic. When you secure yourself in a healthier environment, the advice would be to try and restore peace, which I think is very rare in such a family but possible. Nonetheless, if peace is unattainable, then I would completely cut them off and avoid them. It is good to pray for them to find peace within their hearts. We do not want them spewing evil into society.

Now, if you are in a difficult situation that does not permit you moving away from your antagonistic half-siblings and stepmothers, then you need to find a strategic way of tolerating and ignoring situations when possible and living with them in harmony. Most of all, you must commit the situation to God, because nothing is impossible as long as you have faith.

Marrying Multiple Wives

How could a man expect peace in his home when he single-handedly destroyed that home by marrying three wives? It is already a challenge to coexist with one person in your home, so what were you expecting would happen with two or more persons? First of all, your relationship with one person is automatically changed the moment person number two joins in. You have polluted your bond of trust with the first wife and thereby encouraged a personality disorder in her, which will eventually provoke quarrels and fights. Even if your first wife consented to you taking a second wife, the second wife may come into the family with an attitude of provocation and disharmony, as she inadvertently feels threatened due to her subconscious guilt brought on by her own decision to intrude into another woman's home. This is an invasion which, in the contemporary modern world and even biblically, could only be described as adultery.

There are so many disadvantages that stem from polygamy, more so than the advantages, which are now almost obsolete and most impractical. The utility of many wives and children to help you work your farm, for instance, is now redundant. The farming culture has disappeared. Now, one wife and a few children can be quite a financial strain, let alone multiple wives and numerous children! This is notwithstanding the absence of peace within the household due to warring jealous wives and half-siblings, plus the glaring fact of a bankrupt morality.

Only monogamy should be encouraged in my view, and polygamy should be outlawed. There is a strong element of male chauvinism in this practice, as it turns women into property and the age old excuses of there being more women than men and men doing women a favor by marrying them and reducing the number of spinsters out there is an absolute load of rubbish!

DEATH

Death is an inevitable phenomenon that we must not fear but embrace when it comes to us, especially in the gracefulness of the aging process. Yes, it is the tail end of life, and even though we wish for it not to happen, it must manifest at some point. It is the only certainty of life—death.

However, as human beings, we are naturally afraid of the news or the thought of death, because the finality of it is very painful, particularly when it involves the loss of a loved one.

It is very important to care for a loved one who has arrived at the final stage of life or rather is on the way home. This selfless and noble service of love and care would only lift up their spirit and ease their journey.

Do You Need to Be Drawing a Line?

Question—wife or girlfriend: "Where do you draw the line on your husband's or boyfriend's female friendships?"

When the question of drawing a line arises, there must be a problem of trust and respect between the couple. A relationship built upon the bedrock of trust and respect in addition to other virtues does not require spelt-out restrictions.

The man should know his limit with female friends, because his wife must be considered and her comfort prioritized naturally. In my opinion, it is okay for a man to keep female friends as long as he respects the boundaries of decency and morality. He has to discipline himself to maintain self-control and remain sensitive to the emotions of his mate.

Drawing the line is usually hard work for men in general, as their physical animal instincts are quite powerful when it comes to lust of the flesh. They are easily seduced by the beauty and attractiveness of the opposite sex and are hard pressed to resist temptation, unless they are in touch with their spirituality. No matter how much they love their wives, fiancées, or girlfriends, they must strengthen their resolve to be monogamous by constantly refueling their spirituality.

Personal Transformation

I think we all do need a makeover at some point in our lives, because career choices, work, and challenges have a way of causing self-neglect or demanding an alteration of some sort to either suit the job or to harmonize one's personality.

Personal transformation can actually be fun if it enhances one's lifestyle and attracts positivity, so let us embrace change in our personal lives.

Giving The Audience Something Not to Be Bored About

Many need another person's downfall to feel better about themselves. That is why ongoing scandals about celebrities, for instance, fascinate the public and sell fast while the subject's brand thrives.

However, we must make a difference by turning that trend around by having happy inspirational endings that uplift the spirit and make one feel even better about themselves. That's a given lead to enhancing one's self-esteem. The demonstration of a controversially positive brand and the development of excitement about good and creative phenomena to stimulate the imagination of the public and propel them to higher levels and aspirations should be the order of the day in the future to encourage the public to prefer good news over bad news, as opposed to the other way round where the media habitually focuses on sensationalizing bad news rather than good news which the public are taught to find boring.

Beware of Small-Minded Jealousy

When you suffer from small-minded jealousy, there is a tendency to pick on people for trivial reasons and peddle stupid little gossip. I want you to know that your mediocre personality becomes quite glaringly obvious when your warped, uncontrollable jealousy finds it difficult to contain itself when threatened by your own insecurities and ignorance.

Many wise people become aware of your shortcomings, and they may choose to just sit and listen and to analyze you for their own personal reasons. Even if they are not alert enough to grasp your deficient personality, the moment they experience any personal challenges with you, alarm bells will ring in their spirit, and you will be reacquainted with that very moment in the past where you acted frivolously by badmouthing someone else to them. Beware!

Getting Frustrated Often?

Frustration is a natural human inclination when one experiences struggle and failure, but it is very dangerous to one's mental growth and stability, so we must be cautious of how much and how often we allow ourselves to get frustrated and be careful not to wallow in it.

Yes, frustration can influence one's judgment of people and things in a negative way and may even cloud one's vision to actual progress or positivity.

Thus, it is indeed critical to caution oneself about giving in to frustration in times of disappointment.

Know Yourself

Understanding who you are should have a great influence on your decisions. Knowing who you are can be interesting and gratifying if you have a healthy self-esteem. You spend less time on mundane concerns and more time nurturing yourself and pursuing your goals.

But when you find yourself less satisfied with who you are, it is imperative to reevaluate your life and perhaps seek therapy. Self-deprecation is usually the inclination when one is dissatisfied with oneself, but it hampers one's happiness and deters one's growth and success; therefore, it is better and rather effective to pursue knowledge and build your self-esteem, leading to healing and growing to reach your potential.

Ambition

Ambition fuels one's life. Your aspirations should dictate your daily activities. What kind of life is a life without objectives and challenges? Pursuing a goal keeps you busy and propels your emotional and mental growth. It is like a task that puzzles your mind and provokes you into deep thinking that will in the process enlighten you and thereby reveal critical information too. This process also consumes time, energy, and focus, which will allow little or no time for you to engage in the nonsensical, such as malicious gossip. Therefore, it is right to say that ambition can also spare you from the negative drama that looms up in idle minds.

Ambition propels one's destiny! If you aspire to be significant to your world, then there is the tendency to discover your strength that is your purpose in life. The process of creativity reveals talents and great qualities. The passion for that creativity drives your daily activities, thus projecting you into society and thrusting you upward to greater heights, maybe even further beyond your imagination.

When you can share your talent with the public, you are driving your energy upward, and then consistency only springs you even higher. Do not be afraid to challenge yourself. You will be surprised at what you are actually capable of. Everyone has a purpose, so find yours!

SOLITUDE

There is peace in solitude. And, of course, solitude allows for a deeper reflection into life that can reveal substantive messages and clarifications of life's challenges. As a creative writer, I also realize that I am able to create better when I am in solitude. To create amidst other spirits, they must be happy spirits, spirits that are flourishing in their realm and can also coexist with other spirits. Lost and angry souls can only cause vexation in one's spirit and thereby cloud one's vision. One cannot be creative without a vision. Good vision can only be revealed to a focused and clear mind. Focus and clarity is obtained through tranquility.

Steering clear of distractions helps you realize your ambitions.

Enjoying One's Own Company

Being able to spend time with yourself keeps your spirit calm and at peace. Such an activity is a virtue, and it allows you to reflect on your life to understand where you are and to evaluate your achievements. This will also be a real basis to realize your full potential and give you an insight on how to explore it effectively.

It is okay to hang out with people you enjoy and be with people you have to be with, but you have to be able to go back to your home, to your serenity, because it is the only place that allows you to ponder deeply into life and be at peace with yourself and the rest of the world.

It is not a very good thing to crowd your home often. Even though sometimes you want to have family and friends over for merriment and companionship, it is not good to do that all the time, because—as I said earlier—that the spirit needs its own serenity for reevaluation and planning. These virtues are difficult to explore in a crowded environment.

You can have one or two happy spirits at home that truly resonate or are in tandem with your spirit; not to say that there will not be some disagreement or misunderstanding, but these types of good spirits are always willing and able to cultivate friendship, peace and love, so there will really never be harsh issues, just an environment of nurturing.

Be in Tune With The Spirit

It is very critical to be in tune with the spirit, as your destiny may be confronting you at any moment in time, and if you are not alert, chances are that it would elude you. And then, you will continue seeking and wasting energy and time in the wrong places with the wrong people who probably seem right without the insight of the spirit.

I am trying to say that the key to your destiny may be with the person sitting next to you on the plane. It may be with the market woman that you are so shamelessly arguing with publicly for trivial reasons. Be alert. The other people and doors that you may believe are the right connections and are very focused on and hoping and waiting for something to happen may not really be the divine connections you need. You should always be alert to new developments and the actual reality of different situations.

It is also true that seemingly appropriate or right people and doors may be the stepping-stones and not stumbling blocks after all, as their activities are likely to be keeping you afloat and focused on your journey and may also inspire another perspective and reveal different dimensions to your journey that may not have been discovered, had you not indulged them.

Having said that, you still need to be alert to not spend more energy and time than is needed with such people, because that could eventually become disastrous or a real encumbrance to your destiny.

Gift of The Gab

There are people who are blessed with the gift of the gab and are usually very suave and eloquent in speech. They have optimum communication skills, but for some strange reason, most of the personalities who possess such a gift use it with bad intentions and hardly for good.

If only they could employ it for positive things and by doing so create a better world around them.

Perhaps such persons should commence self-evaluation, which I think is necessary to work on uplifting their self-esteem. Yes, darling, only a low estimation of oneself can provoke the use of such a gift to dupe others for evil gain.

INSTINCTS

Your instincts cannot always be right, because life's challenges will affect your emotions and consequently reflect in your thoughts. Your natural feelings are subject to the confusion caused by the harsh realities of life. Even just a colleague's or a loved one's mistake can confuse your mind and cause you to become irrational about any issue you try to analyze at that point in time. It can just become confused and rather impulsive!

Good instincts are mostly in harmony with a healthy state of mind—the mind that is in tune with the spirit. The thoughts and decisions conceived in such a mind are usually in alignment with God's will. When you align with God for your life's journey, then He can communicate with you through anyone and anything, and your instinct harmonizes to His messages.

Potential Dangers in Surrogacy

I think it is healthier for a couple seeking a child to adopt as opposed to a natural mating or insemination with a surrogate mother. Why? I'm skeptical and practical for a few reasons; surrogate mothers, unlike those that already gave up their children for adoption, are yet to live the experience of surrogacy. They may have decided to embark on that journey mostly because of financial difficulty. It is impossible to predict how you would feel with a child growing inside of you. It is impossible to know how you can go through the bonding with a child over the nine-month process. After birthing and perhaps breastfeeding, which cements the bonding, you then give the child up to another family. The discomfort and pain of breaking that bond may cause the surrogate doubts about her decision.

In some situations, surrogate mothers may also begin to have expectations of the man as a result of the ability to give him and his wife a baby. Yes, as emotion plays a major role in every facet of our lives, it is certainly a factor in this situation and even deeper in effect if a baby is involved. One usually expects the parties to avoid sentiments and focus on the business at hand, but you may not be able to control the emotions. Such involvement may stir up if the surrogate mother experiences a deep chemistry with the man or vice versa. Of course, there must be a certain level of chemistry between the said man and the surrogate mother for them to even initiate mating to conceive the child. Now, there is a tendency for that journey to spiral to a complex point if the surrogate mother is single and free of external obligations that may have been compelled by a boyfriend or husband.

Therefore, investments in surrogacy must have clearly defined understandings.

But since adoption is not an option for many people, as they are almost always skeptical about the breed and character traits of the child—most men prefer their bloodline unless they are infertile—then that option is excluded. In such cases, I would advise that employing insemination with a surrogate mother is less complicated.

Absentmindedness

Absentmindedness is a negative state of mind. Why does one need to be absentminded when consciousness is an embodiment and the core of life? One who is absentminded is depleted of energy, sensitivity, information, awareness, and focus, and these virtues are required to experience the nuances—the real elements of life. Even the challenges that build the character within you elude your absent mind, as you are not alert to seek the treasure obscured in each challenge. Yes, there is a treasure concealed in every challenge we collide with, but we must seek that treasure to find it. That treasure may simply be an idea, or a clarification for a past event, or information to the pathway of a big success, or even a certain level of understanding, patience, and strength required for greater future rewarding events. It could be anything but always a life-changing factor.

We must rebuke this evil spirit of inattentiveness. We must be attentive to our environment and ourselves so that we can learn and grow and revel in every aspect of life.

Unrealistic Expectations From New Mate

Unrealistic expectations from your new relationship and your comparison of your new mate to your ex tend to provoke in your mate a personality disorder and is even more dangerous when it happens at the onset of the relationship while you are still dealing with the person's representative. When you meet someone, you are not really meeting the "authentic person." You are meeting their representative. This is because every human being have the natural inclination to want to prove worthy of the object of their desire. Naturally, we all tend to wear the mask of perfection in the beginning of a relationship, because we want to prove worthy of our mate. Only time and event can crack those masks. Now, forcing out a personality disorder in addition unmasking the representative is definitely a disaster waiting to erupt.

It is healthier to allow yourself to experience some of their good qualities by being loving and caring. Those good qualities are likely to serve as a balance or encouragement to tolerate your mate's flaws when they are eventually revealed. Someone's good qualities can help you to tolerate their flaws, if those flaws are not overbearing.

Forget Seeking A Perfect Mate!

There is no one without flaws. A perfect or ideal mate is one whose flaws you can tolerate. You yourself have flaws! Your ex-partner had some flaws, and the new mate also has some flaws that should be revealed with time and challenges, but do not provoke them deliberately by your unrealistic expectations and comparisons.

Whenever you compare your ex to your new partner, it should be for the sake of growth and not for spitefulness toward your current mate. Telling yourself that you are doing better with your life and decisions or that you need to do better and not go backward or repeat past errors is the result of a healthy evaluation and reflection. Learn to live in the present and experience the "now" so that you can savor all there is and have more clarity and energy to relish the future.

Letting Go

You must try to move on from your past relationship, so that you can experience every nuance of your new relationship. Your new mate can never be exactly like your former relationship, because they are two different people traveling their respective individual journeys, so you must desist from comparing them or expecting the new mate to behave like the old one or to treat you in the same manner as your ex treated you. If your ex was your perfect mate, they would still be in your life, right? Naturally, like everyone else, they must have had flaws, which most likely caused or contributed to the breakup.

An unrealistic expectation of your mate does have a negative influence in your judgments of their deeds, and that negative influence also reflects in your actions toward your mate. If you are treating your mate with less than they deserve, then you will be treated less than you may deserve as well. Every action has a reaction, and what you offer determines what you inspire or elicit from others. Thus, if you treat your mate with antagonism, you will provoke antagonism; if you treat your mate with selfless love, then you should also inspire their selfless love.

If your new relationship is clearly very problematic, then the prudent action is to discontinue it. Lingering in a difficult or even toxic relationship and complaining and making foolish comparisons will only compound your life's problems.

Yelling When Angry is a Natural Human Inclination

It is only human and impulsive to rave, yell, and talk stupid when one is angry, but there are people who would either recede afterward and not persist or would dwell on the fight and even harbor anger toward their antagonist. I think it is rather wise and healthy to retreat, as harboring anger is a burden unto the soul and a reflection of weakness. It also means that the other person still governs your soul from a distance. Oh yes, if you sit there gossiping, sulking, and whining about your adversary or supposed contender, then they are in control of your soul, whether you like it or not. Why should you allow anyone to be in control of your soul and indirectly cause obstacles for your future when that anger you harbor toward that person will inevitably and unconsciously influence almost every facet of your life in a negative way?

Of course, continuous fighting and anger seems natural and appeasing to the minds that are unrelenting in controversy. Okay, whatever you please, but be aware that you will also suffer alone, since the other person has most likely progressed on to better and more beneficial activities.

Unburden your soul for your own good! Be wise and take the high road to freedom and fulfillment!

Explore Your God-Given Talents

God has given us everything we need to fulfill our purpose, but it is left for us to recognize those qualities and explore them.

Often, we look outward for our glory, but it should rather be projected from inward to the society. Yes, when you recognize your gifts and celebrate them, you will be rewarded for them.

Remember, people can only celebrate you when you can celebrate yourself, and you celebrate yourself by sharing your gifts with society.

Disturbed Spirits

Most times, I wish there were few or no disturbed spirits trudging through society, but then again, this is an elusive dream. Unfortunately, it is a far cry to desire that peace will reign in our communities; for our economy to be healthy; for there to be structure and balance in some countries so that they do not project chaos onto the rest of the world or pollute other countries where there is already a certain level of balance, law, and order; to desire a healthy environment, one with very little or no pollution from waste products like petroleum and diesel; pure and clean drinking water; unprocessed and healthy food; perfect medical and health systems; security; and so on. Nonetheless, we must persistently wish, pray, and work hard strategically to achieve such a virtue of excellence in our society.

Clearly, the lack of those aforementioned conditions is the cause of most disturbed souls. Yes, I believe that strongly! The spirit becomes stifled by struggles, failure, disappointments, illness, and other disasters one collides with in life. That repression can plunge the spirit into virtual oblivion and consequently obscure dimensions that keep one further away from reality. Hence the "crazy" people you meet—the constantly "angry" people you collide with, those who snap at every triviality or even misconstrue a kind gesture—may be victims. Yes, when one is in darkness, judgment of people and things is mostly warped!

Okay, do you know that disturbed souls will only multiply in number, as they are likely to pollute more souls with their warped minds? Yes, because when a disturbed soul meets a weak or vulnerable soul, it can easily provoke the weak to ruin. Weak and vulnerable souls happen to be increasing in great numbers, as the world is plunging further into darkness due to wars and natural disasters rampantly sweeping across some parts of the globe, even without warning, defying human intelligence, science, and technology. It is almost like we have approached the end times; perhaps we really are at the end times, because the occurrences in the world at the moment seem to be reflecting the revelation in the scriptures.

Some disturbed souls are caused by evil spirits; yes, there are evil spirits in our society that prey on the vulnerable and weak souls until they take control of them. Agents of darkness are eager to destroy the children of God!

Some of these weak and vulnerable spirits emanate from a bad foundation and not always from struggles, affliction, failure, etc. One's foundation can influence one's growth and journey in life. Oh yes, darling, even in times of crisis, the confidence and discipline instilled in you and your spirit of prayer can carry you through. Thus, it is important that parents ensure they raise their children in a healthy, God fearing, and prayerful environment, as it will be the structure for the lives of their children and continuously radiate light along their path.

Wish

A wish can be a mechanism to actions that can translate to success. It can only be healthy to wish good things, though some people just wish and do little or nothing about their wishes. If the wish is able to translate into imaginations, it has the tendency to manifest to reality if the subject of imagination is kept alive in that realm long enough to begin to instinctively influence one's actions that tend to propel that wish to realization. I am simply saying that we could manifest our great wishes if we can invest energy, focus, time, and action.

I wish to be a voice for change. What is your wish? May you wish for positive things, and may they also come to fruition.

Structure and Balance

Structure and balance are the two major features of a progressive organization and even a nation, so one must work on the basic construction of a plan and stabilization to propel success. To develop a proper formation and balance, there must be a solid foundation, as it is almost impossible to build on precarious ground. However, if there is uncertain and unhealthy ground, it can be reconstructed and solidified to support the type of structure one needs to erect on it, though it requires comprehensive assessment, patience, strategic planning, even using scenario thinking and a steadfast course of action.

For the best results, of course, you need the right architect with a healthy imagination and the right inspiration to create your vision. This administrator will then assemble the right team to realize that vision. Persistence is necessary in structuring and balancing the project, because these phenomena are usually not achieved swiftly or rarely even on a projected timing, as errors are almost always made and corrections are therefore needed in the process to gain the anticipated results. Proper planning can minimize trial and error, so think your plan through and "measure twice and cut once" for the most efficient use of time and energy.

New Goal

New goals require a new attitude, because your perspective is soaring toward a new dimension. This means you need to reevaluate your attitude, clean your environment, and make plans that will propel your new concept.

There is a tendency to look back at past failure and fear some repetition, but remember that apprehension has the propensity to generate negativity and unnecessary distractions in the spirit that will unconsciously influence your judgment and environment and consequently manifest the disaster you dread. The memories of past failures should only be revisited for reevaluation to avoid repeating mistakes. Remember that dwelling on failure is the failure and not really that you failed in your quest. As we know, if you are attentive, your failure should lend you different perspectives to life around you (your environment, abilities, and capabilities), so be sure to utilize that lesson in your new goal.

One key to success is a positive attitude, so you must not adorn the robe of skepticism.

Your failed method, in some cases, still can be implemented in a new goal, but you must make a clear assessment to be sure that strategy does apply to your new goal and actually has been successfully utilized by others in the past; otherwise, it will be another failure.

Peripherals—A Distraction

You must try to seek the root cause of your problem and not be distracted by the peripherals that you encounter, because they tend to delay your journey or deter your progression in unraveling causes and seeking effective solutions.

There may also be greater challenges ahead that require that time, energy, and focus you are investing in, so do not waste it on trivialities. Sometimes, that triviality may seem like the real challenge because of the situation surrounding it that may be in concert or even resonant to your basic dilemma, but be very thoughtful as you may just be peering in the wrong direction as a result of weakness or strong ulterior motives or in some cases desire for revenge, if it applies.

Evil Act Has No Limit

There is no limit to an evil act. One evil action consequently births many other evil actions. Once you commence evil, the spirit that governs that evil multiplies in action to veil its initiator and to reinforce its effect. Then, the initiator is at the point of no return, with no room for repentance, and the complexity of the problem cannot be resolved. You find yourself plotting more evil to conceal the previous ones. Your spirit plunges deeper into darkness, and your sense of morality deteriorating by the minute. Your vision of people and things distorts.

"Over My Dead Body!"

Really? Do you seriously mean that? Something happening only over your dead body? If it is fate that it shall come to pass, then you will definitely die, because it must come to pass, whether you are living or not. Especially when you prove to be an impediment, God will annihilate you to manifest His will. Be careful trying to frustrate destiny, because you will eventually lose. Death does not only mean giving up the ghost but being alive yet stagnant in the spirit and insignificant to society. Be warned!

Do You Want Your Presence Or Absence to Be Celebrated?

Your presence is celebrated when you make a difference in the life of those around you. You impart knowledge. You are creative. You are sensitive toward humanity and work to help yourself and those around you. You share even the little you have with those in need and those around you. You prioritize other people's problems before yours. You pray for other people's success and happiness. You even go beyond your abilities and capabilities to solve other people's problems.

Your absence is celebrated when you exhibit a few or all of the following qualities: greed, failure, malicious gossip, jealousy, and evil spirit, and you are peevish, a nuisance, or a sponger.

Falling in Love With Your Tormentor

I try to understand the incidents where a woman who is kidnapped and held hostage for whatever reason would develop feelings for her captivator. Can that be possible? Naturally, when two people spend time together, in spite of the circumstance, their minds tend to desire interaction of some sort. Perhaps out of curiosity, anxiety, or even anger. When there is a mind to mind interaction and experience to whatever level, people begin to yield to a certain extent. Now, that interaction may reveal individual personalities, perhaps with good and bad qualities as well. This process tends to allow the minds to fuse with the quality each person may have inside, though it can also give the mind the opportunity to rebound in criticism.

The scenario where there is tension is expected to naturally preclude or be depleted of the phenomenon that can birth the virtue of love. However, the human mind is complex and unpredictable with matters of the heart, depending on one's grasp of a situation or resonance of understanding of the occurrences or the connection of the victim and the captor.

Almost every kidnapper may have a good person lurking inside, and they may have resorted to crime out of desperation. Now, that is not to justify evil actions, but some people are inclined to irrational actions during desperate times, although that action may vary from person-to-person and depends on their environment, associations, mental, and emotional state. It can all lead to meetings of minds that no one could predict. The intricacies of life!

Noisy Environment and its Negative Effects

Some people claim to lose focus in a noisy environment, while some minds can actually filter through the noise and stay focused. I discovered that noise, depending on the type and source, may actually be an inspiration or be soothing to the mind. I, for example, flow in my thoughts with gospel music or Lucky Dube's songs that are soulful. Others just have the ability or are just so motivated that they can filter out even loud noise and just focus on a task that is vital to them. Professional athletes who say they get so inspired that they do not even hear the roar of the crowd show this. Meanwhile, some others have so-called rabbit ears, because they are bothered by even small noises and do not do well under pressure.

This all illustrates the vast range of the human mind's ability to perform, so it is up to the individual to find the best "sound environment" to work in. The greatest inventor in the world works in silence and with a clear desk on one project at a time, as he has found that complete focus brings the best results. If you feel you must have some sound or music, it has been proven that playing classical music is the sound that will result in the fewest mistakes, as the 4 × 4 beat is the only one that is in sync with the mind. Some people will say they must have "their music" playing when they do certain kinds of work, and they may enjoy themselves more and keep working longer and do fine if the work is not detailed and subject to making mistakes. As with many things, "to each, their own," but make sure "your own" is really the best for you and those around you.

Even the most brilliant philosophers, those with sharp, analytical minds, can be confused in their judgment at a time of crisis, because when the mind is troubled, it becomes difficult to grasp the important nuances of a situation. It is natural for the mind to plunge into confusion, thus missing many dimensions to the crisis. The mind can better grasp the depth of a situation when there is tranquility in the spirit, for peace allows for complete focus and clarity.

Very obvious vital information may seem ambiguous to a confused state of mind. The human mind can sometimes be drawn to the most unimportant information just because it is in crisis, but then at the same time, it may not have the capacity to explore important information and use it to the greatest advantage. I wonder about the human mind a lot!

Irrelevant Advice

There is some advice that is not pertinent to one's condition, yet someone is eager to dish it out. Have you asked yourself why certain people deem it necessary to offer you random negative advice? Why indeed, if not that they are miserable and seeking company or are soulless people who relish in polluting other people's spirit with bad news?

The negative or not so positive occurrences in your life could be exploited to create the bad news, as that could make for easy correlation. That advice suddenly seems relevant to you, just because it resonates with your dilemma. It is easy to provoke paranoia in a person whose spirit is already confused by life's challenges.

It is advisable to pause for deeper thinking and better understanding before considering such advice. In fact, try to analyze your advisor or a gossip to better understand their motive. Like I earlier said, the person may be miserable and seeking company or may just be one of those who need to inflict suffering on others to elevate their spirit. Psychopaths!

CHAIN OF KINDNESS

It is a belief that when you are kind to one person, then that individual should be kind to others, and that builds an endless chain of kindness. However, it is not always the case, as there are people who do not have an iota of compassion in their spirit and are not open to show kindness even when they receive from others. Such people usually feel entitled to what you offer them out of your pure good will, even when they are not deserving of it. Therefore, being kind to someone does not necessarily build a chain of kindness, but you should still be kind without expecting a return, as compassion heals pain, gives hope, uplifts the spirit, and inspires long life and even prosperity!

Chain of Evil

A chain of evil may not be built through victims. There are victims who would not allow themselves to be provoked to evil, even if they are suffering, and that is how we all should be, as evil will only diminish one's spirit and rob one of one's destiny. Though only a few victims possess the spirit of forgiveness, while many may call to heaven for revenge, it is imperative for victims to understand that there is a forceful spirit of justice that governs the cry of a victim, so those who inflict upon you will surely pay, as there is no peace for the wicked. Even if you forgive them, they will still pay for their sins because karma balances life. They may only escape that judgment of karma if they resolve their evil deeds and cry to God for forgiveness.

Treating others with wickedness as a result of your horrible experiences tends to build a chain of evil, as most people are swift to retaliate or react negatively as a result of bad experiences. Thus if I, for instance, react to your evil toward me by treating—for example—James with evil, every action has a reaction, and you cannot dictate the reaction. Evil actions tend to provoke evil reactions, and that can only escalate to unforeseen detriment. Therefore, James would most likely react to others with wickedness as well and even to a higher degree. Whoever James expressed his anger toward may also react in a more intense manner than what James may have done.

One needs to be very careful about this. In fact, one needs to be vigilant, because the world will only flourish with a chain of kindness and not with the chain of evil.

Do Not Let The Evil Ones Change Your Good Heart

Do not stop being the special person that you are because "witches" are restless. Continue being kind and generous, because those are the attributes of a quality soul, and such qualities attract good things to you. However, steer clear of those souls governed by wickedness. You do not need them for your happiness or your progress. In fact, they are only a nuisance, distractions, and tear at your flesh. It is imperative to seek spiritual insight in order to discern these agents of darkness in your immediate environment. The devil is a cunning bastard and would manipulate the people in your close vicinity to poison your soul and subsequently alter your good and superior attitude to mediocrity. Yes, mediocre and weakened is what your soul becomes when you yield to wickedness and turn away from goodness.

Do you know that wickedness is darkness? Wicked people are deformed in the spirit and tread on crooked paths. They cannot appreciate straight and seamless roads to real life and happiness, because they are warped. They revel in pain, failure, and war. They find it impossible to feel joy. They cannot appreciate life and happiness, even though they make believe they know what they are and pretend to need them. You cannot appreciate life and happiness and relish in wickedness and anger.

The Contents of Your Soul

The contents of your soul could determine the condition of your physical body as well as your disposition or projection of life. If your heart is angry or stifled, then subsequently your body's potency would decline, and your flesh would rapidly age or decay, in spite of what you eat or how much.

The contents of the soul can also cause obesity of the mind or even cause you to gain unnecessary weight, as you eagerly and ignorantly eat unhealthily due to depression. Some people seem to find comfort in food, even bad food. Some people begin to ignore their physical appearance, because their minds are too repressed, angry, or polluted to process healthy information. If your mind is contaminated, your dispositions will reflect negativity and even low self-esteem, as that ugliness in your soul would inevitably distort your judgment of people and things and thus eventually reveal your flaws.

Liberate your heart from anger and bitterness, as it is the governor of your being, and you cannot flourish in the spirit or in the secular world while wallowing in anger and bitterness.

Are Your Energy and Skills for Destruction?

Isn't it amazing how evil people seem to have the energy and skills to destroy but not to conceive great ideas and pursue meaningful goals to achieve success? The world would be so much better if only they could channel that energy into helping themselves and making themselves relevant to society.

Associating With Failure Can Lead to Failure

If you want to keep progressing, steer clear of those that keep failing. Failed spirits are not necessarily those who just failed but those that wallow in failure.

Failure is a component of growth, but growth can be deterred by dwelling on failure. You are inclined to failure if you are associating with failed spirits, because their spirits are weak and polluted, and thus nothing fruitful can emerge from them. Rather, they will continuously plunge deeper into failure and try to drag you down with them by their words and actions. If you dare try to help them, you are asking for trouble. They hate you for having the ability and the willingness to help them, and they want to blame you for their weakness and failure. They suddenly see you as rivals. They cook up stories to create enemies for you, because they are simply losers and, of course, there are always willing souls for enmity, so those are easily convinced, as they also have their issues lurking somewhere in their hearts that are influencing their judgment. They pretend to love you as long as you are giving them money or material gifts, even though they may hate you with a passion and wish you would disappear.

Incident of Insensitivity

Someone may know that you are in some dire situation or are struggling to achieve something that has proven difficult for you, or you may even be on the path of healing and trying to seek salvation, yet they deem it necessary to feed your heart with bad stories, because they are out for revenge against another. Ridiculous if you think this person loves you and has come to be your special friend, because they couldn't care less about your feelings and are rather interested in their mission to inflict harm on another.

Unfortunately for you, your not-so-special friend is a selfish "witch" who only wants to inflict you with emotional pain, and God forbid it escalates and becomes detrimental to you, as emotions play a major role in every facet of our lives. If you are emotionally stifled, then your judgment of life will be distorted. That pain will unconsciously affect other areas of your life.

If this person does really love, respect, and consider you, they would be more sensitive and cautious of the stories they tell you or peddle about you. Obviously, you have not been considered, hence the evil stories and attempts to stir up hysteria. Be wise!

No Common Sense?

Common sense is relative to an individual's understanding. Your mind makes common what it can conceive, but that does not apply to others, as they may also be struggling to grasp the concepts of your analytical mind.

A broken soul is mostly inclined to irrational thinking. One cannot expect a repressed spirit to conceive logical thoughts.

Do You Underestimate Your Potential?

Do not underestimate your potential, for God instilled in each of us talents to develop and pursue meaningful goals and realize our purpose in life, which gives meaning to our existence. All you need to do is look inward and understand who you are and discover your unique talents. When you discover those talents imbued in you, do not be afraid to explore and build on them to the best of your capabilities. You will be presented with many challenges, so do not shy away from them, as they will give you different perspectives on life and can also be your personal "school of hard knocks." If you learn your lessons well, they can propel you to success.

As humans, we have the tendency to doubt our strength during life's, trials but that spirit of doubt is simply our enemy that is likely to create stumbling blocks for us, so we ought to rebuke it immediately and proceed with faith.

Spirit of Leadership

Very special are those who are birthed into leadership in the spirit. Most are simply elected into leadership, but very few are born to be leaders. The personalities that are just elected leaders have proven to lack the full appreciation of the position they hold, while the very few born leaders project the spirit of leadership in its entire form. It is often done by instinct, with real vision and inspiration.

Looking Down on Someone

Be careful! You may miss out on opportunities and help from a friend or family member just because you look down on that person, do not appreciate who the fellow is, and are hypocritical, pretending to like the person but peddling malicious gossip and spewing evil comments against them at will.

We tend to take our friends and family members for granted, just because we have the opportunity to have the closeness that lends us enough insight into their private lives. You can only have a good grasp of an individual's shortcomings when you are familiar with that person. We must not allow familiarity to breed contempt.

Communication Between Couples

Communication is the basis of a healthy relationship. Communication builds and sustains a relationship. How? Couples must communicate their thoughts and feelings to each other to understand each other's weaknesses and strengths so that considerations are tendered fairly and squarely where needed.

You cannot be unhappy and then suppress the feelings with the hope that it will be okay, whereas that suppressed feeling has the propensity to influence your behavior. Emotions play a very major role in every facet of our lives, so if a person's emotions are stifled, they will inevitably have a negative effect in the fellow's subconscious mind and thereby influence their actions during interaction or even cause a disinterest and subsequently provoke unnecessary problems.

Your mate is not a soothsayer and therefore can never know or grasp your exact feelings and thoughts unless you communicate. Whether good or bad feelings, it must be communicated in some manner. Now, the manner and tone of communication is also vital to build, heal, or sustain a relationship. Therefore, couples must adopt a healthy approach to communicating their feelings and thoughts, as the ultimate goal should be to stay together and be happy with each other.

Communication also helps couples to appreciate the nuances of their relationship so that support and encouragement are tendered where and when necessary. Planning and future goals are also shaped accordingly. Therefore, if you and your partner know your singular and unique style of living and navigating life, you should factor them into your decisions and choices to pursue goals and arrive at a mutual agreement and understanding that helps the both of you reach your full potential.

A couple's alignment in their goals and decisions eases their journey toward building a successful relationship and leading a fulfilling life together.

Challenges Reveal Weaknesses

Struggles, challenges, and failure have a way of repressing your spirit and revealing your weakness. However, do not be despondent, for those are the elements of life that build character in you. There is just stagnation in a spirit that has not been challenged, so you cannot appreciate life and all its intricacies or realize the will of God for your life.

However, you must not wallow in those disappointments. You must analyze what went wrong, learn from your experiences, release all blame and shame, raise your level of expectations, and—with the help of the Holy Spirit—rekindle the greatness within you so that you can take positive action to ensure your success.

The Splendor of The Concept

The Finished Work

Have you ever wondered why the workshop is always behind the show room?

Friends, the reason it looks like you are behind your peers is because you are still in the workshop. God is still working on you. You are still under construction, and as soon as God is done with you, you will be at the show room for your world to admire, appreciate, and reckon with the finished work.

Unconscious Limitations

Everyone has some sort of limitation, from physical to mental and even to the extent of one's vision. However, there are also the self-imagined and evoked limitations that emanate from the consciousness of a person. Your insecurities and fears and even past failures individually or collectively seed or impose limitations on your unconscious mind.

Unconscious limitation is a bondage that you must unshackle yourself from and embrace life from a higher ground where there are endless possibilities coupled with an awareness and light.

Weave Wearing and Fake Hair Loving is Not Particular to Black Women

Now, those of you who say Africans are trying to be Americans or be like the Westerners, I want you to know that Africans are not the only people crazy about fake hair or extensions. I live in Beverly Hills and have lived in many countries and always in a Caucasian or Jewish community. Most of my friends wear hair extensions and even wigs. They are not Africans or women of color. Fortunately for them, people tend to believe it is all their natural hair, because their choice of hairpieces is always natural to their own hair, unlike the women of color who will wear straight, silky hair and other hairpieces that are not akin to their natural hair texture.

HELP

A person may need help but not accept there is a necessity for help or want to be helped!

To gain assistance starts with accepting that there is a need for it and making oneself available to it. It is almost always a waste trying to offer help to persons who are not willing to receive it. If you are so eager to assist such a person, then the effective approach would be to first hold a mirror to show the person the deteriorating state of their situation and hope they would perceive it and thereafter avail themselves for assistance.

Naivety

Sometimes, it is good to be innocent and inexperienced, because you can be excused for errors, and there are those who would gladly run to your rescue or who feel fulfilled when they are needed by a pretty, naive girl. But many times, and in most situations in life, it is important to have knowledge and wisdom, as these are necessary tools to lead a safer and more fulfilling life.

Innocence and naivety may be cute initially, but sooner or later, maturity—a consequence of experience—prevails.

The Fire Brigade Approach

It is amazing how people just sit around for weeks, or even months, when they know they have an important appointment for whatever reason at a particular date and time, telling themselves (and others) that "there's still time," "we have plenty of time," then suddenly a few days before that same time, there is a scramble to make preparations and meet up with the requirements. Unrealistically high expectations are placed on those who are involved in the project, and woe betide anyone who fails to meet up with the deadline. Sometimes, they are deprived of funding, but have to find a way around it anyway, or else . . .

Even worse, a few days before an appointed date, skilled hands who have a time schedule in which to practice their respective trades are told that they have two days to complete a job of two weeks, or else!

Why do we like to put ourselves in a tight corner? The job situation forces the unfortunate graduate or professional to take up the challenge. And what happens? The end result is mediocrity! Rushed work—badly finished! And everyone wonders why things are never done properly in some places.

Do You Have The Ability to Survive and Thrive?

Prospering and survival, depending on which is applicable to your life, should be paramount in everyone's life. Many of us dwell in an unhealthy environment, whether by choice or not, and the majority of that number only want to survive and are not even interested in thriving, as it requires catching a vision, creativity, and harder work to prosper in life.

Hard work also requires self-discipline, which is an elusive phenomenon in a dejected soul. A depressed spirit is devoid of the energy that strengthens and drives the mind into conceiving ideas and cultivating self-discipline required to work, hence the reluctance to prosper in the spirit of those who settle for just surviving.

Think of thriving! The thought of doing something inspires one to make a move, and the interest to act on the subject of interest becomes the drive, and thus there is a potential for success.

Can we go past the thought of just surviving and push ourselves to prosper?

Communication in a Relationship

Communication is very important in a relationship. Things that are unknown normally are perceived from a negative angle. For example, the husband says, "I met this great lady . . ." and so on and so forth, and the wife thinks, "What's he up to, now?"

The quicker the mate can meet this person to see with her own eyes, the better it would be. The fact is, the lady he describes to her may not even be the type of woman he would date, but if she never meets her, then the speculation becomes "my man met the most beautiful and the sexiest woman . . . My man is this and that," and so it continuously bothers her.

Knowing someone is having an open healthy communication.

The Downfall of a Man is not The End of His Life

So you have lost all your wealth, and life has not been fair to you. So what? Should that end your life? Does that kill your talents and passion that should recreate wealth for you? Was not the success a result of hard work, focus, and persistency that you could readopt to revive your situation?

Failure ought not kill one's talents and zeal for life; it is merely a temporary setback. Failure should be appreciated for the lessons and growth it engenders in a person's life. Yes, failure lends us a different perspective to life while strengthening our spirit. It is not how hard you fall but how well you rise when you do that defines your strength, and thus the healthiest reaction to failure is to endeavor to rise above it. Do some reflection into your journey to reevaluate your steps and decisions to understand how you arrived at the point of failure. That process should reveal most of your mistakes to you so that you can take the necessary corrections.

Most people believe that failure reflects weakness, ignorance, and stupidity. That could be true in some instances, but failure is also an element of everyone's growth, and those aforementioned pathetic reflections of failure can be attributed to each and every one of us at some point in our lives. Should we now expend time and energy cutting ourselves down when we have failed? No! The latter action is indeed the failure itself, because you are not a failure because you failed in a task but a failure because you dwell on the failure and destroy your life in the process.

Mediation

Mediating between a couple obviously gives one an insight into the rupture between them; nonetheless, that confidence does not in any form give you the right, nor is it ethical to divulge the contents of their sorrow to someone else or to the public.

The sole reason for your role should be to salvage the relationship by restoring peace accordingly and by not exacerbating the problems. Persons with weak minds are known to exploit such situations for several reasons that are certainly lacking in substance and destructive in consequence. We must not capitalize on other people's challenges or betray the trust put in us.

Do You Wish to Become Someone Else?

Be appreciative of who you are, because there is a special person in you.

Yes, God has molded a special person in every one of us, but we must look within to get acquainted with that unique personality in us. Instead of asking God why you can't be like the handsome Jim and pretty Joyce, instead of becoming fixated on the rich and famous people, why not spend that time and energy thanking God that you are alive and ask Him to help you discover the astonishing talents and great energy He has instilled in you?

If fame and excess wealth are not within your reach or attainable in your choice of career, then you will never attain them. But that does not mean you will not strive for the success that you are meant to achieve. You have your own purpose to fulfill and must work toward it. Wallowing in self-pity, dwelling on failure, looking down on yourself, and comparing yourself to others are collectively self-destructive habits.

YOUR INFINITE POTENTIAL

The power of self can also be gained through self-discovery and by understanding one's weaknesses and strengths. It seems easier to realize one's weakness and wallow in self-pity than it is to discover one's strength and capitalize on it.

Struggles and challenges tend to void our potential, but you can rekindle your infinite potential when you learn to take control of your challenges. You will be more in tune with your capabilities when you are balanced in your spirit.

Life Force

Your focus on your success, on the beautiful things in your life, or on your great goals strengthens your life force. In other words, positive energy empowers your spirit. I notice that when I am angry for any reason, my spirit declines and represses my enthusiasm for creativity, work, and even socialization, unless I am alert and decide consciously to channel that energy to things that are productive and beneficial to my growth and success.

I believe that my inherent understanding of who I am and my need to pursue my great goals compels me to snap out of anger. And then to achieve a positive state, I talk to God in a short prayer, or I listen to music that is soothing to my soul.

It is important to have a good grasp of your personality and to know you have a purpose. Understanding these factors should help ease your anger when necessary, as nurturing the spirit of anger is destructive to your life.

The Destructive Element of Words

Sometimes, the strong adjectives or demeaning phrases said to a person, to express an opinion about them or to describe their flaws or limitations can be destructive to their soul. If only we could look for alternative words that are not cutting and demeaning but would still convey the corrective thoughts and will therefore motivate the person to look into the problem and pursue healing.

Physically Nourishing The Spirit

Have you ever felt your body coming to life and connecting with your soul?

Being extremely healthy in your body and appreciating the feeling it sends to your soul is a very strong connection we all need to gain in our lifetime. How can we achieve such a condition with the struggles of life and even the destructive components of our nutrition that we are ignorant of because we pay little or no attention to the type of food in our bodies, the inevitable effects it has on our mind and thoughts and actions, and how it can diminish or prolong our lives?

Yes, if we can pay attention to our health and try to connect it to our soul, then we are on our way to leading a healthy and fulfilled life.

I have come to realize the positive events that occur in my life when my body feels good and my soul is happy. It gives me a sense of satisfaction that encourages me to indulge in positive activities. However, my spirit tends to decline to its lowest factor and lose its functionality when I feel sick in my body.

Now, it is difficult to caution oneself of the quality of food one consumes even randomly because of lack of time and convenience. It is rather more demanding to exercise the body to maintain a healthy physique and release the accumulated stress on the muscles. However, we must endeavor to adopt the discipline needed to practice this healthy and rewarding lifestyle.

I stretch even when I'm too tired to work out!

To Fight is Sometimes to Die

Death does not necessarily mean to give up the ghost but to also deplete the spirit of light, to darken the spirit. Do you not know that when the heart is clouded with evil thoughts, the soul that governs it declines in potency? Yes, when you fight a war or plan to fight in one, your spirit loses its energy, and your mind and spirit gravitate toward negative and evil activities such as killing, death, and destruction.

Fighters naturally believe that they have control over their evil actions against another human being, but that is a delusion, as one cannot dictate the reaction of the fellow being attacked. The negativity of your evil actions will generate will inevitably spiral out of your very own singular control.

Since we live by the dictates of our mind and spirit, we must keep them healthy, else we become self-destructive through our warped judgment and actions and the extensive consequences of inflicting harm on others.

A dark spirit is depleted of the authority and dominion required to govern one's world, which is then mentally, emotionally, and physically enslaved.

Your Woman's or Man's Evil Friends

Yes, those evil friends who always seem to have the most negative and unfruitful advice for your mate. They are all over the place, meddling into relationships of others and eager to be relevant, though they have nothing tangible to proffer to heal or help build a relationship.

Every relationship goes through some sort of struggle, and the duration of that challenge only depends on the couple's collective willingness and their ability to overcome. Absolutely! There must be a collective desire and effort from both people in their relationship to solve the matters that are challenging them.

That effort can be encouraged by the friends that we keep, because there is the human tendency to share our private matters with friends, but then again, it could produce a bitter result as we may be asking the opinion of a polluted spirit—a friend who only seems to perceive evil and negativity and will only proffer a solution from such a weak source.

Thus, we must be careful of the type of friends we choose to share our challenges with. It is healthier and safer to approach a professional therapist, councilor, psychologist, or even a psychiatrist, because such professionals are there solely to help you find effective solutions to those formidable problems.

The Effect of Listening in a Relationship

Listening allows us to achieve a greater understanding of life and of our environment, and it is even more effective in building a healthy relationship.

Good communication between a couple or even between friends is achieved through listening.

Actually, when you listen with your ears as the instrument of your heart, you will gain a deeper understanding, because the heart is where compassion lies. If it is the basis of your understanding, it will go to the core of your being and encourage a healthier response from you.

Reevaluation

Sometimes, you should stop and make a conscious effort to reevaluate your life so that you can gain necessary perspectives to your surroundings, decisions, and goals and thereby be inspired with the needed clarifications to move forward. You could even gain revelations to prepare for the future.

It is impossible to lead a successful life without having a good grasp of your environment and goals and without reviewing your actions so that change can be enforced where it is needed.

Courage

Courage is fearless.
Courage is doggedness.
Courage is bravery.
Courage is a propellant.
Courage is a forward moment.
Courage is a magnetic force to success.
Courage is inspired energy.
Courage is inclining to the future.
Courage is heroic.

Courage is believing there is hope.
Courage is believing.
Courage is having faith.
Courage rekindles you with the greatness within.

Courage is an elusive phenomenon where there are challenges and excruciating struggle.

Courage is a strength that we all must summon at some point in our lives to rise from failure or to pursue success.

To Heal Someone Emotionally

To heal or help stabilize someone emotionally is an immense task that requires wisdom and mental strength to achieve. It is not easy to address other people's emotional issues, and it is even harder to offer an effective solution to their problems, as the person may feel embarrassed with the content of their trauma and may want to share the lighter part of the problem only or give you a substitute to the truth of the matter.

Since the intention is to heal, as a motivational speaker, I have realized that people are more willing to allow me to help them, because I am eager to share my own struggles to let them know that challenges are not particular to them and do not make them less of who they are.

In essence, for you to offer a real solution to a person's problem, you ought to encourage the truth in that person by possibly sharing your own challenges and the steps you have taken to resolve them.

What Kind of Future Would you Have With a Violent Mate?

Even though we wish for a long and lasting relationship, even though we believe we should grow old with our choice of mate, life's complexities tend to propose otherwise. Every perfect and imperfect relationship is predisposed to change, and we must learn to yield to change accordingly and with caution, so that we make a decision prudent and effective for progression.

Unfortunately, the change I address now is one that tends to destroy and even more so demands vigilance and wisdom.

Your partner may have been the best person in the world with great qualities that were suitable for your ideal mate. You probably had the best experiences in your lifetime with your mate, until things began to change due to one awful situation or the other. Now, you may not be the cause of that unappealing situation, but your reaction to it could have escalated to all the problems you are now having with your mate. It could also be that your mate is the only one responsible for all the problems, because they are too weak in heart to apply caution and wisdom in dealing with them.

Everyone is in possession of both good and bad qualities, and it is a fact that some people may seem like they wear theirs like a garment, as whatever quality is dominant in their spirit is often evident; however, if the bad trait is the silent and inconspicuous type, it also has the propensity to sprout with life's challenges. When that evil trait emerges without caution, it tends to flourish with energy from a toxic environment. The constant arguments at home, nagging, antagonism, etc., are examples of the bad energy that pollutes the environment and subsequently encourages the monster within your once perfect mate.

What do you do in this situation where vexation now governs the heart of your mate? It is not wise or healthy to dwell in an environment that is toxic to your soul. Fatality is very strong possibility in a relationship where violence is the order of the day. Therefore, you must consider dissolving the relationship to save your life and perhaps that of your friends and family members if they, out of concern for your safety, are entangled in the web of that violence, too.

There is no future for you with a violent partner!

Your Mate Straying Away From You

All the qualities your mate once appreciated about you are suddenly insignificant and therefore not thrilling, anymore. Your partner begins to stay out more and stay away from you as often as possible. Your company or even a little concern of how their day went is perceived as an intrusive control. You become an irritant and a thorn in your mate's flesh. Opinions offered by you lack substance, and your efforts and assistance rendered to your mate are not appreciated.

Yes, your mate is seeking an outlet for those stifled emotions, and they spring out with a little opportunity. How did this all happen? How did the spark between the both of you suddenly varnish? You obviously do not have the foresight to discern this kind of challenge in your relationship. Perhaps you do have a little clue as to what is happening, since you may have triggered it and lost control of the relationship as a result?

This is what I am thinking: Couples tend to be vulnerable to outside influence when there is an unresolved issue between them. It is almost natural to seek comfort from an available stranger when your relationship with your mate is declining. Then, the new lover may be very compassionate and willing to be there for you as much as possible, thereby creating room for a deeper level of emotional connection.

Your mate may have found this type of comforter who now is their scapegoat. Ouch! You are in trouble, because the growth of their relationship only widens the void between you and your mate, and in fact it unconsciously provokes your mate's ill temper and influences their actions and reactions toward you. The electrifying chemistry your partner may have with this new friend will surely eat deeper into your relationship with your mate, causing an eventual, bitter dissolution of your relationship.

What are you doing to salvage your relationship? Do you want to restore the fire that once burned between the both of you, or are you tired and would rather move on?

If you wish to heal your relationship with your mate, you should start now and not wait for it to dissolve first, as it may be more difficult then.

We are all Different

We are all born with a unique individual difference from each other due to the biological makeup to our physical structure, thoughts, actions, and dreams.

It seems to be a human tendency to fear or resent a person who possesses a look, character, or ability that is not usual or does not conform to what is termed to be conventional, even if they do not pose a threat to others in any way. Nonetheless, it is wrong and can be appalling, as we are inclined to treat those unique personalities we deem weird with derision. Imagine the sorrow we subject these people to! Imagine the destructive conditions our abhorrent behavior can compel our victims to, and perhaps even provoke a personality disorder that may affect the people that cross paths with them.

I believe that ignorance, weak spirit, and low self-esteem are the factors that dictate such awful behavior in a person who views a unique personality as a problem. We must understand the fact that not everyone can be like us and learn to appreciate the distinct difference in others.

You do not have to interact with a person you deem weird. You do not have to even look in their direction or comment on their lifestyle and activities. The outstanding personality that you think you have would conform to the aforementioned principles. Investing time and energy in exhibiting awfulness toward a unique personality only reveals the evil in you and will inevitably evoke evil upon your life.

Charity Begins at Home

You cannot govern a state, preside over a country, or hold a position of authority and leadership in any sector, if you cannot govern your family, which is your immediate environment. You will not be dealing with animals but human beings, and it is important to understand the difference between the two and know that the teachings and corrective methods employed with animals differ from those employed on human beings who are said to possess five senses, deeper thinking abilities, emotions, and a higher level of sensitivity.

"Charity begins at home" is not just a mere axiom but a real factor in the journey of life. Yes, your lifestyle and the principles you practice at home will extend to your outside world. This means that how you live at home is how you will conduct yourself in public. The same principles you practice in your personal life and the way you conduct your private dealings will be employed in your dealings with people in society. You cannot give what you do not have. What you give may be from an idea conceived by you or a concept you willingly adopted from someone you know in your private life who shared their conception; therefore, it is important for us to be cautious of our lifestyle and personal principles with the knowledge that their effect is extensive.

What is The Real Cause of Your Problem?

We are likely to look in the wrong direction for the cause of a problem when we are confused, because a perplexed state of mind is inclined to distorted judgments and, even more so, is unyielding to real facts and would thus reach the wrong conclusions, even though they may seem right at the time.

Therefore, it is helpful and prudent to allow the mind to calm down for clarity; without comprehension, one cannot recognize the root cause of a problem and would not find effective solutions.

Depths of Your Soul

Your character, imagination, and understanding are formed in your center core. Your soul can project darkness or light, depending on the substance that is felt through your disposition, so it is important to be in tune with your spirit. This is so you can reevaluate the contents of your core from time to time, which is vital, as we are subject to constant changes in our environment and in our challenges. These are the inevitable events of life and often have the propensity to cast dark shadows on our soul and thereby affect our imagination, understanding, and personality if we do not take positive action and use our mental abilities to keep on the path to success.

Your Eagerness to Succeed

Your enthusiasm for success inspires the vision you need to achieve success. No one achieves real success without goals, passion, and hard work. Yes, the wealth bequeathed to you by family, the one achieved through divorce, or ill-gotten wealth are not the type of success that truly illuminates and fulfills the spirit and inspires quality growth in those who will idolize you.

Your eagerness to succeed compels your day-to-day activities; it orders your footsteps and dictates your lifestyle and even unconsciously influences your attitude toward friends and associates. I realized that when I discovered my talents and began enjoying my progressive creativity, I withdrew from many friends and became more selective with those I associate and spend my time with. I now value my time and energy to the point that I find it stupid to expend them on people and things that are lacking in substance and cannot add value to my life.

I rise each day with plans and tasks to accomplish, and I work very hard toward achieving them. I no longer take things for granted. I am not absorbed by my beauty—even though I do highly appreciate the masterpiece God has made out of me. Yes, I look after myself to the best of my ability, because it is necessary and healthy to do so. My ultimate desire is to achieve my goals and fulfill my destiny, not to live up to the stupid, unrealistic expectations of people but the purpose for which I was created.

Success is relative! Purpose is life. Do not live your life trying to achieve other people's dreams and wishes for you unless they are in alignment with your purpose and goals. Do not live a life of stagnancy; your eagerness to succeed is nourishing to your soul.

Hold Firm to Your Great Ideas

Your negative experiences may cause you to believe that your ideas no–matter how practical and unique—are unattainable. A jealous friend may also discourage you, because they do not want you to succeed. It may also be that the friend discouraged you simply because they cannot grasp the substance in your vision.

There are a few other reasons that may deter you from realizing your vision, and you must try to understand the dynamics of the ideas you conceived to prevent avoidable pitfalls and challenges. Yes, it is important that your idea is realistic! Is it applicable to your environment? Is there a market for it in your area? Does it require you to change location? Some of us operate in a wrong environment, hence the stagnancy or failure in our career. Some of us may be in the right environment but lack the attitude needed to navigate that environment. Are you mentally and emotionally and even physically capable of pursuing the goal you have set for yourself? Do you possess the technical knowledge required?

You may also be approaching the seemingly right people who would cost you time and even money, but in the end you may realize the door you walked through was wrong, and you are suddenly in despair and reluctant to move on. Let me tell you something about that. That is also a very destructive element to your personal growth, as you are likely to ensnare yourself into danger because of your vulnerability due to failure and despair.

Hold firm to your unique and practical ideas. Do not lose hope. You must continue to strive for success. Keep trying all you can and even beyond your strength, because your passion will also encourage the people you meet to appreciate your vision.

Remember to align yourself with God, your creator, for He is the maker of greatness. Your faith in Him will eventually inspire your efforts to fruition.

Jobless Critics

These are the critics who seem to know how you ought to live your life and how you should dress and act, even when they are clearly confused about their own lives and are miserable. Their flawed style is glaring and is not even appealing, yet they think they are experts at fashion and eager to tell you how to reevaluate your own style.

No one is in this world to live up to anyone else's expectations, and it is only by chance that two people can find compatibility or can appeal to another, so you are ignorant and delusional if you run around expecting people to act to impress you or to live up to your unrealistic expectations and be sequestered into the box you have carved in your weak soul.

In my opinion, you must not befriend or pay attention to people whose lifestyles and attitudes do not fit in with yours. Remember, someone else would find you unattractive just like you deem others unfit to gain your appreciation. I have learned to look away if someone or something is not pleasing to me and would not even expend my energy making silly comments as long as the subject or person is of no threat to me.

The lifestyles strangers on Facebook or Twitter and blogs display cannot detract from your very own life unless you willingly emulate any destructive elements of their exhibition or spend enough time on their walls to unconsciously absorb what display. Yes, the latter is very likely, because what you read and hear constantly tends to unconsciously influence your life, so if you are feeding your mind with negativity, then you are disposed to the destruction that is adjunct to it; if you are feeding your mind healthy messages, it will have a rather positive effect on your life.

Steer clear of the walls of people you do not like on Facebook, because their actions are inconsequential to your growth if you are aware of who you are and what you need. Do not expend your time and energy passing strictures on them, because you are insignificant to them.

Pregnant for a Man Other Than Your Husband?

Why would you even want to complicate your life, marriage, and future in such manner? How do you expect to get away with that abomination? What could possibly be your reason? If you are not happy in your marriage, which I suppose may have been the reason for the infidelity, you could have opted for marriage counseling or divorce where the relationship cannot be salvaged. Yes, divorce, because that would be a healthier option than infidelity, and that which results in the birth of a child outside marriage is unforgivable and can be extensively destructive.

Some women may think it is a sin that can be concealed, but I say it is a delusion, because nature may take its cause by afflicting the child with an illness that would require the biological father's help by donation of blood, for instance, thereby exposing the secret.

This is a very sensitive issue that can complicate the lives of all your family members, including the child in question. Imagine the stigma the child could suffer at school if their peers get to know their foundation? We all know that the socialization aspect of a child's life exposes the child to the strength and weakness of other children, and in this instance, the child's stigma may kindle with the weakness of other children and provoke them to bully the child.

It is imperative that caution is applied to prevent such complex and deadly situations.

Life is Forward

Forward thinking is a rebirth of hope; a gravitation to light. Forward thinking unravels the mystery of life. Forward is progress! Forward movement gravitates you toward a new environment, thus introducing you to a new world.

Sitting with a straight posture projects your image forward, thus revealing or encouraging confidence; and we all know that confidence is a propellant to life and happiness. Therefore, even a reflection of it in your posture can attract good luck to you. Forward vision escapes you from the bad memories of yesterday and compels a new experience. It moves you ahead as opposed to behind. In actual fact, "forward" is the way to go.

Parents, Try to Listen to Your Children

Parents must try to cultivate healthy relationships, or at least share quality time with their children so they can have heart-to-heart conversations that will allow their children to open up about their personal private challenges.

Do you know that you and your offspring will evade so many unforeseeable problems by sharing a close friendship? Yes, if your daughter—for instance—can confide in you about her relationship issues, that will give you the opportunity to guide her as best as you can. If your son can approach you with his challenges at work or in social situations, you should be able to offer him some good advice to confront those challenges and thereby prevent worse issues.

As a parent, you are a big part of your child's growth, and you should therefore set the pace for your child's success.

It is hard work to be a parent, but it is rewarding to be a good parent.

Only a Foolish Boy Abandons His Pregnant Mate

Yes, a real man of substance does not deny his pregnant girlfriend. Only an inferior, cheap, and immature boy runs off refusing to take responsibility for his actions with flimsy and illogical excuses. Suddenly, the woman is a whore with several partners and only trying to pin the pregnancy on you. Oh, and she is blackmailing you for whatever reason, or she is not good enough for marriage or for your support. The humiliations you meted out to her out of wickedness cannot even be supported.

Men, if she is good enough for sexual intercourse, then she is deserving of your attention, care, and support when you impregnate her. You were in ecstasy during that intercourse, so obviously she was not a whore or a blackmailer at that point in time.

Ponder on your evil actions deeply, because there will be a divine punishment on a day of reckoning. There is a forceful spirit of justice that governs the cry of a victim, and when you eventually collide with that karma, it will be at an unexpected time of your life.

Unfortunately, the sins of the parents do visit their children, and the curses you invoked upon your life may thus fall upon your innocent children, if you have them.

Learn to take responsibility for your actions. A man who abuses and exploits women is the lowest of mankind.

Your Purpose

Purpose is the key to bestowing your unique gift upon the world. My goal is to inspire the hero in you.

The journey to realizing your purpose in life discovers and projects the hero in you, your strength of character, and your significance in the world.

Every man needs constancy of purpose to live a fulfilling life. It is impossible to lead a life of fulfillment when you focus on things that are not in alignment with your destiny. Wealth cannot fulfill the spirit; only the realization of your purpose can bring fulfillment to your spirit.

Living From Your Essence

When you can live from your essence, then you will be free of hate toward yourself or others and all the evil behavior that burdens the soul and generates more evil and inevitably invokes bad luck.

Learn to walk in a higher frequency, a higher vantage point where there is wholeness and liberty. Let your worries—when you have any—be focused on the need for harmony in the world and not in the nonsensical that only reveals your inferiority complex and bitterness.

THE WICKED SISTER-IN-LAW

Sometimes, I try to understand the awful attitude of sisters-in-law to their brothers' wives. Is it that they committed a crime by getting married to your brother or that you just cannot fathom their love and what may be driving their relationship to the point where it is flourishing? Does their perfect relationship cause you misery and provoke within you the spirit of jealousy? Is it that you are a sadist who cannot afford to see those around you happy?

Do you realize that someday you would also be wearing the same shoes as your sister-in-law? Has it ever occurred to you that your mate's family members may not accept you, or are you a soothsayer that can foresee what will happen in future? I would like to know how you plan to avoid or confront the likeness of you in a bad sister-in-law if and when you do eventually get married!

Guilty sisters-in-law should be aware that their evil actions toward in-laws would only invoke the spirit of justice that will manifest in different ways in their lives.

The Dawning of a New You

You must be open to an evolutionary change when you understand your purpose and catch the vision, as you then have to build from the power of resonance to create your new world. The Dawning of a New You births a New World around you!

Everyone has some greatness in them—indomitable attributes that need to be discovered—but you have to be open to it, be vigilant, and tap into your gift. It will emerge if you are alert and tuned into your spirit, and you will then be able to give it your best.

Well-Being

Many of us are oblivious to the significance of well-being and that the inevitable opposite result is unhealthiness, which may be due to culture or simply ignorance. I know that most of our homes and families—as Africans, especially—are not configured to address such a basic necessity. I am also very sure this deficiency is common in many other cultures and families, and it should be addressed accordingly using modern intelligence.

Well-being comes from our chi (or spirit), and our chi emanates from our body and mind. Thus, well-being is based on our state of mind. One must have a healthy and vital life-giving belief system, because being well is much more than just your body; your thoughts, your core beliefs, your feelings, and your actions and inactions all contribute to your state of mind and therefore to your well-being.

Hope and faith are part of our well-being. Optimism elevates the spirit; it is like euphoria for the soul, and when the mind is free of worry and fear, one's thinking ability is healthy and usually productive. Your decisions will resonate with your actions, and those actions are likely to yield very positive results.

Forgiveness and understanding leads to well-being. If you do not forgive, how can you be well? You are repressing your spirit by holding onto pain or inflicting suffering on others. Bitterness has never solved a problem and forgiveness does not, in any way, reflect weakness on your part and does not mean that you are encouraging your adversary's folly or crimes or even that you must continue associating with them. It is even more sensitive when the issue is between siblings or couples.

Those of you who are prone to abusing your spouse, children, and family members must refrain from such abhorrent behavior, because death may result from it, and it may even be your own. The trauma from abuse will also diminish the abused's self-image and confidence, thereby affecting their basic well-being. Your humanity and love must override your ego, your anger, and your need for control. This is your family, and you should employ compassion and love even when you feel you must correct or even reprimand.

Surrounding yourself with people of high integrity who appreciate you can inspire your realization of self, which inspires well-being. The contrary is diminishing to the spirit. Imagine associating with people who demean you or assassinate your character? Such barbs and humiliations will definitely have negative impacts on many facets of your life, so seek people who are positive and uplifting.

As most people know, the intake of food can promote or detract from our well-being. It is important to eat healthy, and that can range from the type of food we eat to the portions we devour. Eating just food that tastes good or any food that is put in front of us can be dangerous to our health, so we must nourish our body with the right fuel. Many of us do not even know about vital nutrients or the difference between carbohydrates and protein. This is vital to our well-being, so we must endeavor to acquire such basic but important knowledge.

Eating excessively, let alone gorging yourself with food, has many negative effects on your body. The body's potency declines when the stomach is stuffed. Fatigue is inevitable and, as a result, drains your ability to work or engage in important tasks. Your thinking faculty is likely to decline, and you may even become sleepy; even when you do sleep, it may be troublesome, depriving you of the deep sleep necessary for the rest and recovery you need to be at your best.

Many of us just get in the habit or actually think we must take every opportunity to overindulge. In addition to the discomfort and most probable ill health adjunct to such behavior, it is imprudent to be greedy when there are people starving for even a little food, so find a way to share your extra money. You will save with others and promote both your well-being and theirs.

If we understand the significance of our being alive and all we can accomplish, then all the things it takes to maintain and promote our well-being must be prioritized so that we can reach our full potential and create what we really desire.

Comfort in Extreme Poverty

It is puzzling that there are actual persons who find comfort in extreme poverty, as they find material things to be an encumbrance. Living in a well-furnished or just a comfortable home can be an obstacle and a restriction to their mobility. They want to be able to move around from place to place without worrying about anything. They would rather live on handouts and beg than have a career that is most likely going to require a skill, creativity, hard work, respecting protocol, a certain level of self-discipline, a long and constant interaction with a chosen group in the company etc. Even self-employment requires hard work, and these are demanding factors on their weak person.

Creativity, hard work, discipline, and protocol are all healthy components of human growth and should not provoke fear or enhance insecurities. Avoiding them is plunging into oblivion and darkness.

Can We Try to Get Along? or Do You Relish Conflicts?

Social interactions will be free of resentments and conflicts when we begin to use our ears and eyes as the instruments of our heart. The heart is the custodian of compassion, and kindness will thus be the basis for our actions and communications, and we will be in harmony accordingly.

Anger Over Nonsensical

Why would you want to burden your soul with anger for something nonsensical? You magnify trivialities, because you are at war within and are thereby unconsciously seeking outlets to express or release the anger that is consuming your weak soul.

Be careful, because the spirit of anger can be extensively disastrous, and you most probably cannot undo most detriments that result from anger.

Character Flaw

Character flaws are the negative elements of human behavior that have the propensity to deter one's growth or impede one's success in career, marriage, friendships, and interactions with people in general.

Now, what overwhelms my analytical mind is how someone may have a completely different opinion about the same alleged character flaw! Yes, another person may actually find the same habit you condemn to be appealing. Why? Because their culture, experiences, environment, desires, mental and emotional state, grasp of life, etc., are different from yours, which are the factors that could collectively influence their opinion. So, because you deem someone's character flawed does not necessarily mean that others will agree with you!

Suffice to say that the alleged character flaw may not necessarily be an impediment to the bearer, since it is limited to each individual's perception, unless of course, the person with the character flaw is dealing with the one with the negative viewpoint.

The intricacies of life!

Limitation

A limitation or a restricting flaw is not as bad as we usually believe. Yes, it may really feel awful to fail in a desired goal or a given task or to be rejected because of your shortcomings; however, I actually think that—like imperfection—limitation is human. It is a growth-aiding phenomenon, and the failure it causes in your life can be turned into a stepping-stone if you try to seek the lessons there are to learn. I would advise you to focus on seeking that treasure and to not dwell on the failure.

It is definitely human to cry and feel disappointments, but wallowing in that pain will not heal or change your fate. Instead, it will deepen your hurt and provoke more challenges in your life.

Natural Hair

Yes, I understand that natural hair breaks in harsh weather and needs to be treated and protected. I have and am still experiencing it in my sojourn to Africa.

Yes, I know that hair breaks with medical conditions and thereby demands an artificial hairpiece as an alternative. I went through this battle during my skin graft surgery because of all the medicine I was taking after surgery.

Yes, I know that we want to change our looks and would use artificial hair, too. I do it all the time.

Yes, I know that it is probably easier and cheaper to maintain weave than to maintain natural hair.

Oh yes, I know how much it cost to run to the salon twice a week.

My problem is not that you wear weave! My irritation is that you believe you are only beautiful with weave. That is a contrived thinking and your singular perception, because I—and most people—do not believe one is only beautiful with a weave on. I feel and look more beautiful with my natural hair, in spite of my love and use of wigs.

I do not care what quality of weave you wear or can afford. In fact, I only like to adorn the best of everything as long as it is attainable without me selling my soul for it. The best is also relative! My problem is that you believe you have to wear Brazilian hair to belong to the circle of "big girls." My problem is that some of you have to degrade yourself to buy the Brazilian hair just to belong in the stupid circle of big girls. Poor orientation. To belong in the so-called circle of big girls, I believe, is to add value to society and to achieve your purpose in life and not to just achieve Brazilian hair.

Beauty is a feeling, and that feeling is reflected in your projection and disposition which magnifies your features.

You who construe love of self for superiority and arrogance have a major self-esteem issue. You should learn to appreciate yourself. You who believe a woman wearing her natural hair is a way of degrading herself also need to reevaluate your attitude toward yourself and life. You do not need to have all the materials in the world or to wear a Brazilian hair to feel beautiful or to love yourself. It is indeed pathetic if the aforementioned factors determine your beauty and happiness.

You are entitled to feel the way you wish. However, I advise and urge you to appreciate your natural African hair more than you appreciate the weaves.

Peace Within

Learn to cultivate peace, as it is the bedrock upon which a successful life is structured. A restless or troubled spirit clouds the mind that conceives the ideas to pursue success. Furthermore, it distorts one's judgment of people and things, thus creating confusion, unnecessary deviations in one's journey, and most likely impediments to success as well.

Change

We know that the only thing constant in life is change. Change occurs for reasons known and unknown, planned and unplanned. Sometimes, we succumb to the change even when it is negative, depending on our state of mind and the grasp of the change. Often, though, we are unwilling to take a stride for change or yield to it even when it is necessary, because we are afraid of the unknown and the extensive outcome. Yes, we are usually reluctant to make a change, especially when the prospective result is vague.

However, we should always be willing to make a healthy change to further our lives. Moving out of our comfort zone is generally a risk, because there is much uncertainty that portends to change that is needed to move forward and progress in life. But, as we all know, one can make the wrong decision for change.

The Grace of Perfection in Man

The grace of perfection embodies purity! Little children are the only ones who possess the grace of perfection, as they are yet to transgress or even grasp the meaning of sin. They are not impressed, nor are they trying to impress anyone. They just act natural and do as they feel, completely next to nature. They are truly the embodiment of perfection in man. Even in their mischievous antics, their innocence prevails; they know not what they do! They are without exposure, rather like the newborn baby whose shit does not smell, because they only feed on mother's milk, and the excrement is therefore unsullied and pure until it is polluted with foreign foods.

The same applies to the little child who gradually grows out of perfection.

Rebuilding Your Confidence

How do you build your confidence when you find out that somehow, somewhere, you just lost it?

Oh yes, darling, somehow, somewhere, we all lose it. We are only human with weaknesses as well as strengths. Problems, failure, mistakes—they will all eradicate your confidence and self-worth, but those challenges are the inevitable components of life and the integral elements of our mental and emotional growth. Therefore, we ought to learn to deal with them accordingly.

Try to employ your willpower to rise above those struggles. If you are unable to help yourself, seek the help of someone willing and able to aide you.

Life is not all rosy. There are ups and downs in life, in spite of one's status and aesthetic look. The worse thing would be self-hate or self-deprecation, which only leads to insecurity, depression, and even substance abuse.

Endeavor to regain your confidence, because a lack of it would deter your success and progression.

When you succeed, take the time to celebrate. When you fail, take the time to recollect your thoughts, reevaluate your decisions, and make adjustments to your goal.

The Consciousness of Love

Love is a soul, wholeness in the height of one's consciousness.
Love is a purity of thought toward a person!
Love is an electrifying feeling from the depth of the heart.
"Selfless devotion" is a paradigm of love.
Experiencing the consciousness of love is the sacrifice of personal desires.

Though there is a difference between a healthy love and a destructive love.
A healthy love is a reflection of euphoria.

A destructive love provokes sorrow.

Loving is not limited to a special day! I experience love every single day. Love drives my daily life, so I try to surround myself with those who love me and whom I love back.

Your Girlfriends

What type of girlfriends do you have, and what is the basis of each friendship?

Girls, your girlfriends should be in the position to inspire your growth. Yes, it is good to befriend those who are on the same wavelength as you to avoid unnecessary problems, but you could also have a warped sense of judgment about life that distorts your attitude, which instead requires a revaluation and urgent change to steer your life to a healthy path. In this instance, you do not need friends on the same wavelength; you need friends that have achieved or are striving for success with a healthy attitude.

If I cannot be creative around you, you are not my friend. Yes, I must be able to flourish, whether by creating with you, teaching you, or being taught by you, whichever way I will be fulfilled. If none of these elements of a quality time spent are in exhibition, then you are a nuisance draining my energy and wasting my precious time.

You must understand the rudiments of quality friendship and the necessity of them to aide your growth and guide your path in life. Do not indulge in a cheap friendship. Reject worthless friendships, as they could pollute your soul and deter your journey or even derail it. Who and where are not decisive factors to steer clear from stagnant spirits, meaning it does not matter if your family or home is concerned; you must stay focused and choose a healthy path.

Time is ephemeral, and its fleeting nature demands that we spend it wisely. You realize this factor as you mature, and you become pickier in your relationships.

Passion

Passion is a propellant to success. Your enthusiasm for a subject and your goal determines your attainable height of success. Now, many of us conceive great ideas and goals but lack the enthusiasm to really pursue them. There are people who desire success and actually have the abilities and products to achieve success but lack the passion required to market them by the available and necessary means. Your projection determines what you elicit from or inspire in people. Therefore, if you are selling a product or an idea without underlying expressions of enthusiasm for it, then you do not project its true beneficial effect.

Passion is an electrifying effect that lights up a concept or product.

Passion is a magnetic phenomenon—an expression that can hypnotize people.

Passion is an energy that strengthens the spirit while expressing conviction that sells the product or concept.

Passion is a magnifier that projects a product for exhibition in its best light.

Passion almost always produces quality.

You must build the spirit of enthusiasm within you and employ that powerful principle in what you do so that you can attain the heights of glory!

Growth

Struggles, challenges, and failure have a way of repressing your spirit and revealing your weakness, but do not be despondent, for those are the elements of life that build character in you. There is just stagnation in a spirit that has not been challenged, so you cannot appreciate life and all its intricacies or realize the will of God for your life.

However, you must not wallow in those disappointments. You must analyze what went wrong, learn from your experiences, release all blame and shame, raise your level of expectations, and, with the help of the Holy Spirit, rekindle the greatness within you so that you can take positive action to ensure your success.

My Journey

My journey is laced with the intricacies of life
Confronting inconceivable challenges that are molding and building the character within me.

Traveling the universe with curiosity and liberty of spirit
Embracing diverse personality and culture.

Experiencing life from my essence
Peering through the depth of life
Awed by the complexities of life
Eager to unravel its intricacies
Keen to share my understanding of life.

My journey is full of excitement, passion, and splendor
From a healthy state of mind, I visualize a perfect world I strive to manifest when in my element.

I have come to understand that operating from one's element is a compelling force for growth
A quicker way to reach one's full potential
So I try not to allow the challenges of life
The unrealistic expectations and the dementia of others disconnect me from my element.

My world is vested with reality, fantasy, and vanity
I appreciate and explore them to my benefit and not to my detriment
I am not a captive of fantasy and vanity
But I am a master of illusion.

Delusion cannot be attributed to my character
My direction is clear
My decisions stem from a healthy spirit whether prudent or silly
My actions that are lacking in good judgment aid my mental growth.

Failure, rejection, and disappointments aren't elusive phenomena in my life but are merely catalysts to my growth.

My life is a success story
I have risen above countless challenges and have authority over my life
I am an inspiration for the broken, the victimized, and the underprivileged child.

I have been tempered with time and even sorrow
Incubating in the workshop of the Almighty.

My journey has only just started
My finishing line is the fulfillment of my destiny
My journey will end with a positive legacy

My journey is destiny!

Fans Comments

FAN ONE:

Hey Ma'am,

Hope you are having a great day? I had to send you this message, it's been heavy in my spirit don't know why.

I was reading the story of Esther and you came to mind. Esther was a beautiful woman that the King chose to be his bride. She was a Barbie doll that captured everyone's attention. Very exotic and exquisite. She wasn't like the other women in the "pageant" put together by the king's personal attendants to search for a worthy bride for the king. She was a foreigner, an outsider, whose appearance was simple but breathtaking. The king chose Esther on the basis of her looks, he chose her for her beauty and I am sure her sensuality. He wasn't looking at her intelligence, it was the middle east and nobody expects a woman to be smart. But Esther turned out to be something bigger than what she was. Her beauty was a tool used by God to get her in the corridor of power, she was a soldier strategically positioned for what God has foreseen was going to happen to His people. And even though at first she was clueless and scared, she finally rose up to the occasion and won the day for the people of God.

I see you in the same light. You are beautiful and sensual, but every post I have read from you is full of strong messages. You have never posted anything useless.

At first you will be taken at face value, as one of those barbies (I mean this in a good way), beautiful and sexy. But yours goes beyond beauty, beyond sexy. You are smart and not just smart but you got something inside of you. You are a soldier strategically positioned for the end time battle. I don't know why I am saying this to you, but like I said it's been heavy in my spirit the past few days. God is using your looks to get you into the corridors of power for a reason. You possess the key to influence this generation, to impact their thinking. Lots of guys these days think with their manhood (I am sorry I had to say that)! But you are a pawn in the hands of the Lord and I see you are rising to the occasion, you are actually fulfilling what I think is your destiny, touching lives with the word and impacting your generation. My part in your work is to keep praying for you. Please keep doing what you do, if not for anything, for the fact that your post encourages me every time I read them. You take care and be blessed! YOU ARE A GI JANE ON A BATTLE FIELD AND THIS GI JOE's GOT YOUR BACK! Always in my prayers.

PS
Please keep me and my family in your prayers to, I am in Afghanistan.

From a soldier to a soldier,
Leslie

FAN TWO:

BEAUTY FROM ASHES

You radiate so much sunshine, so much confidence, so much love, and so much hope.

Yours is a Beauty from the ashes of a life tainted with grief, despair, and the pains of inequality.

It could only have been love that lifted you from the debris of a chequered life planting your feet on the pedestal of wisdom, grace, and glamour.

You're ensconced in integrity with the fervency of a Champion

I see it with my heart

You becalm me so to speak.

FAN THREE:

Beautiful One

I'm so so proud of you cos you have no pride in you.
You're not vain with your industry; your enterprise stands you out.
You were crafted with finer details, yet you are so down-to-earth, to meet with levelheaded men and see them eye to eye.
I think you have the sterner-stuff, to answer at the gates and match fire with fire if need so require.
You hold your own in every clime with no vaunted arrogance. Your laurels you bring with you with present grace and charm.
You are Beautiful, so so Beautiful in all the ways that count.
If I'm so asked to choose, all I see is you!

WRITTEN BY KELECHI C. NWOSU

Made in the USA
Columbia, SC
07 September 2021